AMERICAN POLITICAL, ECONOMIC, AND SECURITY ISSUES

THE DISCLOSE ACT AND CAMPAIGN FINANCE: OVERVIEW, ANALYSIS AND DEBATE

AMERICAN POLITICAL, ECONOMIC, AND SECURITY ISSUES

Additional books in this series can be found on Nova's website
under the Series tab.

Additional E-books in this series can be found on Nova's website
under the E-books tab.

AMERICAN POLITICAL, ECONOMIC, AND SECURITY ISSUES

THE DISCLOSE ACT AND CAMPAIGN FINANCE: OVERVIEW, ANALYSIS AND DEBATE

DANIELLE P. CACINELLO
EDITOR

Nova Science Publishers, Inc.
New York

For permission to use material from this book please contact us:
Telephone 631-231-7269; Fax 631-231-8175
Web Site: http://www.novapublishers.com

Library of Congress Cataloging-in-Publication Data

The DISCLOSE Act and campaign finance : overview, analysis and debate / editors Danielle P. Cacinello.
p. cm.
Includes index.
Includes reprints of legislative branch documents.
ISBN 978-1-61324-016-8 (hardcover)
1. Campaign funds--Law and legislation--United States. 2. Corporations--Political activity--Law and legislation--United States. I. Cacinello, Danielle P.
KF4920.A25 2011
342.73'078--dc22

2011007695

Published by Nova Science Publishers, Inc. † New York

CONTENTS

PREFACE

The legislative response receiving the most attention to date - and the emphasis of this book - is the DISCLOSE (Democracy is Strengthened by Casting Light on Spending in Elections) Act. This book provides an overview and analysis of major policy issues addressed in the DISCLOSE Act and congressional considerations and implications of enacting or not enacting it.

Chapter 1- As it has periodically for decades, Congress is again considering how or whether to regulate campaign financing. The latest iteration of the debate over which kinds of groups should be permitted to spend funds on political advertisements, and how so, was renewed on January 21, 2010, when the Supreme Court of the United States issued its decision in Citizens United v. Federal Election Commission. Following Citizens United, corporations and labor unions may now fund political advertisements explicitly calling for election or defeat of federal candidates— provided that the advertisements are not coordinated with the campaign. The legislative response receiving the most attention to date—and the emphasis of this report—is the DISCLOSE ("Democracy is Strengthened by Casting Light on Spending in Elections") Act. The House measure, H.R. 5175, sponsored by Representative Van Hollen, was reported, as amended, by the Committee on House Administration on May 25, 2010. The House of Representatives passed the bill, with additional amendments, on June 24, 2010, by a 219-206 vote. Senator Schumer's companion legislation that was first introduced in the Senate, S. 3295, is generally similar to the bill passed by the House. The same is true for S. 3628, a second measure—apparently intended to supersede S. 3295—that Senator Schumer introduced on July 21, 2010. There are, however, some important differences across the three bills, as discussed in this report.

Chapter 2- The Committee on House Administration, to whom was referred the bill (H.R. 5175) to amend the Federal Election Campaign Act of 1971 to prohibit foreign influence in Federal elections, to prohibit government contractors from making expenditures with respect to such elections, and to establish additional disclosure requirements with respect to spending in such elections, and for other purposes, having considered the same, report favorably thereon with an amendment and recommend that the bill as amended do pass.

In: The DISCLOSE Act and Campaign Finance
Editor: Danielle P. Cacinello

ISBN: 978-1-61324-016-8

Chapter 1

THE DISCLOSE ACT: OVERVIEW AND ANALYSIS*

R. Sam Garrett, L. Paige Whitaker and Erika K. Lunder

SUMMARY

As it has periodically for decades, Congress is again considering how or whether to regulate campaign financing. The latest iteration of the debate over which kinds of groups should be permitted to spend funds on political advertisements, and how so, was renewed on January 21, 2010, when the Supreme Court of the United States issued its decision in *Citizens United v. Federal Election Commission*. Following *Citizens United*, corporations and labor unions may now fund political advertisements explicitly calling for election or defeat of federal candidates— provided that the advertisements are not coordinated with the campaign. The legislative response receiving the most attention to date—and the emphasis of this report—is the DISCLOSE ("Democracy is Strengthened by Casting Light on Spending in Elections") Act. The House measure, H.R. 5175, sponsored by Representative Van Hollen, was reported, as amended, by the Committee on House Administration on May 25, 2010. The House of Representatives passed the bill, with additional amendments, on June 24, 2010, by a 219-206 vote. Senator Schumer's companion legislation that was first introduced in the Senate, S. 3295, is generally similar to the bill passed by the House. The same is true for S. 3628, a second measure—apparently intended to supersede S. 3295—that Senator Schumer introduced on July 21, 2010. There are, however, some important differences across the three bills, as discussed in this report.

The bills appear to be aimed primarily at non-campaign actors, particularly corporations, unions, and tax-exempt organizations. The bills propose a combination of disclosure provisions and disclaimer provisions (which are sponsorship information

---

* This is an edited, reformatted and augmented version of a Congressional Research Services publication, dated July 26, 2010.

included within a communication) that would apply to these entities and are designed to give regulators and the public additional information about political advertising that could emerge following *Citizens United.* The legislation also prohibits certain government contractors, foreign-controlled or owned corporations (including some U.S. subsidiaries of foreign corporations), and prospective recipients of Temporary Asset Relief Program (TARP) funds from making certain political expenditures.

The bills do not increase contribution limits for candidate campaigns; they also generally do not address other political committees—parties and PACs. A notable exception would permit parties to make additional coordinated expenditures supporting their candidates. This is the only instance in which the bills explicitly allow for more political spending than would be possible under the status quo.

This report provides an overview and analysis of (1) major policy issues addressed in the DISCLOSE Act, which responds to *Citizens United*; (2) major provisions of H.R. 5175, as passed by the House, and S. 3295 and S. 3628 as introduced in the Senate, versus current federal law; and (3) issues for congressional consideration and potential implications of enacting or not enacting the DISCLOSE Act.

The report will be updated as events warrant.

INTRODUCTION

Political information—particularly political advertising—has been at the heart of American campaigns and elections for more than a century. Throughout the last century, candidates, parties, and interest groups have competed to make their case to voters in the hopes of winning elections and shaping policy debates. At the same time, Congress, regulatory agencies, and the courts have wrestled with how much, and what kind, of information should be available to the public about the sources of those political messages. Questions have also emerged about whether certain actors, such as corporations and unions, should be permitted to participate in elections and other political debates to the same extent as voters. Modern campaign finance policy and law, which emerged in the 1970s, but which built on reforms first pursued in the early 1900s, has responded with a combination of provisions designed to restrict the amounts and sources of funds in federal elections on one hand, and documenting the sources and amounts of funds that are permitted on the other.[1]

Political advertising has both enabled the public to become more informed about campaigns and policy contests, and, perhaps, made it more challenging for the electorate and policymakers to keep track of the various players and issues involved in political debates. This has been particularly true since the 1960s, when broadcast political advertising first became prominent, political professionals began to specialize in media production, and the electorate increasingly turned to television for information.[2]

The latest iteration of the debate over which corporations, unions, and other groups should be permitted to spend funds on political ads, and how so, was renewed on January 21, 2010, when the U.S. Supreme Court issued its highly anticipated decision in *Citizens United v. Federal Election Commission (FEC)*.[3] The DISCLOSE Act, "Democracy is Strengthened by Casting Light on Spending in Elections," which the Committee on House Administration reported, as amended, on May 25, 2010, is the most prominent legislative response to *Citizens United* to date. As with the case itself, the DISCLOSE Act is particularly relevant for the ongoing policy debate surrounding political advertising and its transparency.

This report is designed to provide an overview and analysis of (1) major policy issues addressed in *Citizens United* and the DISCLOSE Act; (2) major provisions of H.R. 5175, S. 3295, and S. 3628 compared with current federal campaign finance law, as shown in **Table 1** at the end of this report; and (3) selected issues for congressional consideration and potential implications of enacting or not enacting the DISCLOSE Act. Legislative developments surrounding the DISCLOSE Act have generally unfolded quickly since the House and Senate bills were introduced. As such, this report will be updated periodically to reflect recent developments and emerging issues.[4]

EVOLUTION OF POLICY AND LEGAL ISSUES

Citizens United is significant because of its potential to change the ways in which corporations, unions, and tax-exempt organizations participate in American elections. Although restrictions on those actors have evolved over time, corporations, unions, and certain tax-exempt organizations were largely banned from spending treasury funds in federal elections for decades. As a result of *Citizens United,* these groups are permitted to use general treasury funds to make *independent expenditures,* which are defined as communications "expressly advocating the election or defeat of a clearly identified candidate" and that are not coordinated with any candidate or party,[5] and *electioneering communications,* which are defined as broadcast, cable or satellite transmissions that refer to a clearly identified federal candidate, aired within 60 days of a general election or 30 days of a primary.[6] Corporations and unions are still subject to the prohibition on using general treasury funds to make contributions to candidates and political parties.[7]

The 1907 Tillman Act, [8] which is considered to be the first major federal campaign finance law, prohibited corporations from making contributions to political parties. With the 1947 Taft-Hartley Act,[9] Congress expanded the prohibition to include corporate contributions to both parties and candidates, as well as expenditures in federal elections. Taft-Hartley also included labor unions in the prohibition. The early prohibitions on corporate and labor union treasury funded contributions and expenditures were included in the first modern federal campaign finance law, the Federal Election Campaign Act of 1971, also known as FECA. [10] The prohibitions are codified at 2 U.S.C. § 441b. In an exception to the prohibition on corporate and union treasury spending, FECA allows for the creation of *separate segregated funds* or *political action committees*, also known as *PACs*. Specifically, corporations and unions can use their treasury funds to establish, operate and solicit voluntary, limited contributions to their PACs.[11] These voluntary PAC donations can then be used to contribute to federal campaigns or to make expenditures that expressly advocate election or defeat of federal candidates.

In the 1976 landmark Supreme Court decision, *Buckley v. Valeo,*[12] the constitutionality of many provisions in FECA was challenged. This case is important because it established the framework for constitutional analysis of campaign finance regulation. In *Buckley*, the Court upheld reasonable contribution limits, invalidated certain expenditure limits, and upheld reporting and disclosure requirements. In addition, the Court created the distinction between *issue advocacy* and *express advocacy*, finding that a communication could be regulated if it contained words express advocacy of the election or defeat of a candidate, which includes words such as "vote for" or "vote against." By contrast, such ads could not be regulated if they only contained general public policy messages that fell short of calling for election or defeat of candidates, sometimes referred to as *issue advocacy.* A generation would pass between the enactment of FECA and the next time that Congress would again enact major campaign finance legislation—the Bipartisan Campaign Reform Act of 2002 (BCRA)—but political advertising and the funding sources for that advertising remained prominent during both legislative debates.

As the legislation that became BCRA was being debated in the late 1990s and early 2000s, a chief concern surrounding issue advocacy was whether the ads were actually about public policy issues—as proponents of the advertisements suggested—or whether they were really messages designed to encourage votes for or against candidates within in the context of ads that were only nominally related to public policy.[13] In an effort to restrict issue advocacy, BCRA created a new concept within FECA known as *electioneering communications* in order to regulate messages that might affect elections, but did not expressly advocate for the election or defeat of a clearly identified federal candidate. Importantly, BCRA prohibited corporations and unions from using general treasury funds to pay for electioneering communications, meaning that potentially any ad that even mentioned a political candidate during pre-election periods would have to be paid for with PAC funds or not aired.

In 2007, in *FEC v. Wisconsin Right to Life, Inc.,*[14] the Supreme Court limited the application of the prohibition, thereby easing some restrictions on corporate- and union-funded ads that would otherwise be classified as electioneering communications. As a result of the Court's ruling, if an advertisement could reasonably be interpreted as something other than calling for a vote for or against a candidate, it could not be prohibited. While this ruling limited the application of the electioneering communication prohibition, it did not expressly overrule it.

CITIZENS UNITED V. FEDERAL ELECTION COMMISSION

Citizens United, a corporation exempt from taxes under Internal Revenue Code (IRC) § 501(c)(4), produced a documentary about a presidential candidate, then-Senator Hillary Clinton. The group released the film in theaters and on DVD, and planned to make it available through video-on-demand and to fund broadcast and cable television advertisements promoting the movie. In Citizens United v. Federal Election Commission (FEC),[15] the U.S. Supreme Court considered to what extent the organization was subject to the federal prohibitions on corporate treasury funding of independent expenditures, electioneering communications, and related reporting requirements.

On January 21, 2010, the Supreme Court issued its long-awaited ruling in this case, and invalidated the prohibition on corporations and labor unions using their general treasury funds to make independent expenditures and electioneering communications. The Court determined that these prohibitions constitute a "ban on speech" in violation of the First Amendment.[16] In so doing, the Court also overturned its 1990 ruling in Austin v. Michigan Chamber of Commerce,[17] which had upheld restrictions on corporate-funded independent expenditures, finding that it provided no basis for allowing the government to limit such independent expenditures. The Court also overturned the portion of its decision in McConnell v. FEC[18] upholding the facial validity of the prohibition on electioneering communications in BCRA, finding that the McConnell Court relied on Austin.[19]

The Court in Citizens United, however, upheld the disclaimer (which is sponsor information included within a communication) and disclosure requirements for electioneering communications as applied to the documentary. These requirements, the Court held, could be applied to the film and related advertisements that Citizens United had produced.[20] According to the Court, while they may burden the ability to speak, disclaimer and disclosure requirements "impose no ceiling on campaign-related activities."[21]

It does not appear that the Court's ruling in Citizens United affects the validity of Title I of BCRA,[22] which generally bans the raising of unregulated, also known as "soft," money by national parties and federal candidates or officials, and restricts soft money spending by state parties for "federal election activities." Furthermore, Citizens United does not appear to affect the ban on corporate or union contributions to political candidates. As a consequence of Citizens United, federal campaign finance law does not limit corporate and labor union treasury funding for independent expenditures and electioneering communications. Corporations and unions may still establish PACs, but are only required to use PAC funds in order to make contributions to candidates, parties, and other political committees.

Congressional Response

Given these developments, questions have emerged about how political advertising might be affected by the Court's decision in *Citizens United* and whether the airwaves will be flooded with corporate and labor union express advocacy.[23] Similar questions have arisen about the extent to which the Court's decision might lead to increased campaign activity by tax-exempt organizations, particularly § 501(c)(4) social welfare organizations and § 501(c)(6) trade associations. Many of the these organizations are incorporated, and thus, prior to *Citizens United*, were generally prohibited from using their treasury funds for independent expenditures and electioneering communications.[24] Additionally, all § 501(c) organizations, regardless of whether they were incorporated, could not serve as conduits for corporate or labor union treasury funds to fund independent expenditures and electioneering communications. In light of the Court's decision in *Citizens United*, some are expecting increased campaign activity by tax-exempt organizations. Additionally, some have expressed concern that organizations might be used as shadow groups—groups to which corporations, other entities, and individuals might give funds to engage in campaign activity with little or no public disclosure.

Because this is the first time in modern history that corporate and union independent expenditures have been permitted at the federal level, it remains to be seen how much additional money, if any, might flow into the political system. A more complete understanding of how *Citizens United* will affect the political environment, including campaign spending, will likely be unavailable until after the 2010 election cycle, at the earliest. Proponents of legislative action have, nonetheless, argued that preemptive legislation is necessary to avoid or at least document an expected onslaught of new political advertising.

LEGISLATIVE ACTION ON THE DISCLOSE ACT THUS FAR

Legislative responses to *Citizens United* began developing immediately after the January 21 ruling. More than 40 bills that are potentially relevant have been introduced in the 111th Congress.[25] The primary focus has been on the DISCLOSE Act. Representative Van Hollen introduced the House measure, H.R. 5175, on April 29, 2010. Senator Schumer introduced the initial Senate version, S. 3295, on April 30, 2010. Senator Schumer introduced S. 3628, a second version of the DISCLOSE Act—apparently intended to supersede the other Senate measure—on July 21, 2010. S. 3628 was placed on the Senate calendar, rather than being referred to committee. The measure would, therefore, rapidly become available for floor consideration.

Although committees in both chambers have held hearings on *Citizens United*, the House has largely focused on the DISCLOSE Act rather than other legislation.[26] Both the Committee on Civil Liberties held hearings to assess the *Citizens United* ruling on February 3, 2010. The Committee on House Administration held two hearings on H.R. 5175 specifically, on May 6, 2010, and May 11, 2010. The committee held a markup on May 20, 2010, when H.R. 5175 was ordered favorably reported, as amended.[27] After the House Administration Committee reported[28] an amended version of H.R. 5175 on May 25, the House of Representatives passed the bill, with additional amendments, on June 24, 2010, by a 219-206 vote.[29]

The versions of the bill as introduced in the House and as passed by the House were generally similar. There were, however, some notable differences. In particular, the House-passed measure modified the bill to

- raise the threshold for prohibiting expenditures by government contractors from contracts valued of at least $50,000 to contracts of at least $10 million;
- clarify that Internet communications are generally not subject to FECA's disclosure and disclaimer requirements, except for paid political advertising;
- require that independent expenditures and electioneering communication reports be filed electronically and in a format that permits sorting and searching data (for reports with at least $10,000 in expenditures); and
- require automated political telephone calls (*robo calls*) to include "stand-byyour-ad" disclaimers.[30]

Comparing the House and Senate Bills

Provisions in H.R. 5175 as Passed by the House, S. 3295 as Introduced, and S. 3628 as Introduced Despite some differences (discussed below), these versions of the DISCLOSE Act would generally

- expand the current definitions of *independent expenditure* and *electioneering communication*, thereby mandating expanded disclosure and disclaimer requirements for certain political communications run by corporations, unions, and certain tax-exempt § 527 and § 501(c) organizations (*covered organizations*), and broadening the kind of communications that may be subject to FECA prohibitions;

- require *covered organizations* to report to the FEC information about their donors (including transfers) and spending for certain independent expenditures and electioneering communications;
- require corporate chief executive officers or other high-ranking officials in *covered organizations* to state their approval for advertising content, similar to current "stand by your ad" requirements for candidate ads;
- prohibit certain government contractors from making independent expenditures and electioneering communications in federal elections; prohibit TARP recipients from making contributions, independent expenditures, and electioneering communications in federal elections; and prohibit corporations subject to certain control or ownership by foreign nationals (e.g., U.S. subsidiaries of foreign corporations) from making contributions, independent expenditures, and electioneering communications in federal, state, and local elections; and
- remove existing limits on coordinated party expenditures if a candidate or candidate campaign does not control the expenditure.

Differences Between the House-Passed and Senate-Introduced Measures

Despite the general similarities discussed above, there are some important differences between the version of the DISCLOSE Act passed by the House and the two introduced in the Senate. Major differences between the House and Senate bills include the following provisions.

- The two Senate bills contain lengthy findings sections. H.R. 5175 as introduced and reported from the Committee on House Administration contained similar findings, but the relevant section[31] was omitted from the version of the bill passed by the House.
- The bills contain different thresholds for restricting independent expenditures and electioneering communications by government contractors. S. 3295 would bar such expenditures for entities holding contracts of at least $50,000.[32] H.R. 5175 as passed by the House would set the threshold contract value at $10 million, as would S. 3628.
- The bill passed by the House also contains a restriction on Outer Continental Shelf oil and gas lessees not found in the Senate bill. The House bill would prohibit entities holding or negotiating these leases from making contributions, independent expenditures, and electioneering communications in federal elections. Neither Senate measure contains such a provision.
- The bills would redefine *foreign nationals*, who are restricted from making contributions or expenditures in U.S. elections, differently. All three measures would expand the current *foreign national* definition to include certain foreign-controlled U.S. corporations, but H.R. 5175 and S. 3628 contain additional prohibitions on entities owned by or under control of foreign governments or foreign-government officials.
- Unlike H.R. 5175 and S. 3628, S. 3295 would revise the lowest unit charge (*LUC*, also called the *lowest unit rate*). Currently, the LUC essentially permits candidate committees to purchase preemptible broadcast advertising time at the cheapest price

offered to commercial advertisers for comparable time.[33] In addition to other revisions, S. 3295 would bar preemption of LUC ads (unless beyond a broadcaster's control) and would extend the rate to national party committees in some circumstances.

- Both Senate bills would require Senate political committee[34] reports to be filed electronically and directly with the Federal Election Commission (FEC) rather than with the Secretary of the Senate. Senate campaign committees, party committees, and PACs currently are not required to file campaign finance reports electronically.[35] The House bill does not address these provisions.
- H.R. 5175, as passed by the House, excludes § 501(c)(3) organizations and certain large § 501(c)(4) organizations from the disclosure and disclaimer provisions.

Table 1 at the end of this report and the following discussion provide additional detail.

POTENTIAL IMPLICATIONS AND CONSIDERATIONS FOR CONGRESS

General Considerations

As Congress evaluates the DISCLOSE Act, several factors could be relevant. It could first be useful to consider what the bill would and would not do. In short, the DISCLOSE Act's provisions are essentially tailored to political advertising—the main policy issue raised by *Citizens United*. In brief, the DISCLOSE Act appears aimed at documenting additional political advertising in general, and restricting it where potential corruption might occur in specific circumstances. Nonetheless, the disclosure provisions would not necessarily affect political spending per se, nor would they necessarily deter those entities that wished to call for election or defeat of federal candidates. As such, the bill would not necessarily ensure an equal playing field among various political advertisers—including campaigns—nor could it necessarily do so.

In general, the bills would broadly apply additional disclosure and disclaimer provisions to entities making independent expenditures and electioneering communications, as defined in the bills. Corporations, unions, and certain tax-exempt § 501(c) and § 527 organizations would all be subject to the disclosure and disclaimer provisions—provided that their activities met the financial and time thresholds required to classify their communications as independent expenditures or electioneering communications. On the other hand, the bills' restrictions on political expenditures apply only to specific kinds of organizations—namely those government contractors, entities subject to foreign control, or TARP recipients falling under the DISCLOSE Act's provisions barring certain political expenditures.

The bills would not, however, directly affect candidate campaigns in most cases. Indeed, the provisions of the bills appear to be aimed primarily at non-campaign actors, particularly corporations, unions, and tax-exempt organizations. The bills do not increase contribution limits for candidate campaigns; they also generally do not address other political committees—parties and PACs. A notable exception, discussed below, would permit parties to make additional coordinated expenditures supporting their candidates. This is the only instance in which the bills explicitly allow for more political spending than would be possible under the status quo.

In addition to the general policy approaches described above, specific provisions in the legislation could be the subject of debate during House and Senate consideration of the DISCLOSE Act. Because the effects of *Citizens United* will be unclear until at least the conclusion of the 2010 election cycle, and because of the quickly evolving debate in Congress, all the bills' major implications cannot be predicted. The following sections discuss some of the potential implications of the bill, which Congress may wish to consider when evaluating the legislation. As noted previously, other issues may also be relevant; additional analysis will be included in future updates to this report as developments warrant.

Maintaining the Status Quo

If Congress chooses to maintain the status quo by not enacting a legislative response, some argue that certain spending by corporations, unions, and tax-exempt organizations to influence elections could go undocumented under current campaign finance law. In particular, it is possible that under certain circumstances, undisclosed funds could be transferred from one organization to another for the purpose of funding independent expenditures or electioneering communications. Those organizations that the bill proposes to prohibit making expenditures, such as certain U.S. subsidiaries of foreign corporations, would also be free to fund advertising as they saw fit. On the other hand, if substantial additional spending following *Citizens United* does not occur, it is possible that additional legislative action is unnecessary. In addition, some might contend that existing law is sufficient to cover many of the topics addressed in the DISCLOSE Act.[36]

Modifying the Definitions of Independent Expenditures and Electioneering Communications

As noted previously, now that corporations and unions are free to use general treasury funds for independent expenditures and electioneering communications, the legislation proposes to document such spending through disclosure and disclaimer requirements—and to prohibit some entities from making such expenditures. The activities to which these requirements would apply depend largely on how key terms are defined. Importantly, the bills would broaden the definitions of independent expenditures and electioneering communications, thereby expanding the scope of FECA's regulation.

Specifically, the bills would expand the definition of *independent expenditure* to include an expenditure "that, when taken as a whole, expressly advocates the election or defeat of a clearly identified candidate, or is the functional equivalent of express advocacy because it can be interpreted by a reasonable person only as advocating the election or defeat of a candidate, taking into account whether the communication involved mentions a candidacy, a political party, or a challenger to a candidate, or takes a position on a candidate's character, qualifications, or fitness for office."[37] In other words, it is possible that an advertisement could be subject to DISCLOSE Act regulation as an independent expenditure even if it does not explicitly call for election or defeat of a clearly identified candidate if the ad can reasonably be interpreted only as advocating election or defeat of a candidate. In addition, the bills would increase the period (from 60 to 120 days for the House bill and S. 3628, and from 60 to 90 days for S. 3295) prior to general election in which communications are treated as electioneering communications. These provisions are noteworthy because they would affect the kind of political advertising subject to regulation under the DISCLOSE Act and, by extension, other provisions in FECA.

Entities Covered by the Disclosure and Disclaimer Provisions

The bills' disclosure, disclaimer, and shareholder/member reporting requirements would apply to *covered organizations*, which would be defined as corporations, labor organizations, tax-exempt § 501(c)(4), (c)(5), and (c)(6) organizations,[38] and § 527 political organizations that are not political committees for purposes of FECA.[39] H.R. 5175, as passed by the House, and S. 3628 would expressly exclude § 501(c)(3) charitable organizations[40] and qualifying large § 501(c)(4) organizations from the definition of *covered organization*. S. 3295 does not contain similar exemptions. Many tax-exempt entities are incorporated and therefore would fall within the definition of *covered organization*, absent an exclusion. Therefore, under S. 3295, the term *covered organization* would include incorporated § 501(c)(3) organizations. It is important to note that the IRC imposes restrictions on the ability of tax-exempt organizations to engage in campaign activity; for example, § 501(c)(3) organizations are prohibited from engaging in such activity.[41] The activities that constitute electioneering under the IRC and FECA are not always the same.[42] For example, it appears possible that an issue advocacy communication, depending on its timing and content, might be an electioneering communication under FECA, but might not be treated as campaign activity under the IRC.[43]

Prohibitions on Making Contributions or Spending in Elections

In addition to its disclosure, disclaimer, and reporting requirements, the legislation contains several prohibitions. Specifically, it would prohibit certain government contractors, TARP recipients, and corporations subject to certain control or ownership by foreign nationals from making expenditures or contributions in connection with federal elections. Table 1, at the end of this report, contains additional detail on individual prohibitions.

Government Contracts

Section 101 of H.R. 5175 as passed by the House and S. 3628 would prohibit government contractors from making electioneering communications or independent expenditures "only if the value of the contract is equal to or greater than $10,000,000." This language appears to suggest that this prohibition is intended to apply only to contractors holding a single contract of at least $10 million.

S. 3295 would apply to contracts of at least $50,000. Although the original House bill had a similar limit, the House-passed bill increased the threshold to $10 million. Some have suggested that this modification was made to exempt small business government contractors from the prohibition. While the value of the "average" federal procurement contract may seem low ($120,634 in FY2008),[44] even small businesses routinely receive much larger contracts,[45] arguably providing one rationale for exempting contractors who have not received a contract

valued at more than $10 million from the proposed ban on independent expenditures and electioneering communications.[46] Agencies may, for example, award contracts valued at up to $3.5 million ($5.5 million for manufacturing contracts) to small businesses participating in the 8(a) Minority Business Development Program without competing them,[47] and some small businesses have received contracts valued at over half a billion dollars.[48] "Large" government contractors, in contrast, can receive contracts valued at over $1 billion.[49]

TARP Recipients and Outer Continental Shelf Lessees

Section 101 of all three bills would prohibit prospective recipients of TARP funds from directly or indirectly making contributions, independent expenditures, or electioneering communications. Notably, it appears that the prohibitions would apply to TARP recipients using TARP funds, as well as their own funds. The applicable period of the prohibition would begin on the later of the commencement of the negotiations for financial assistance under title I of the Emergency Economic Stabilization Act of 2008[50] or the date of enactment of one of these bills, and end on the later of the ending of negotiations or the repayment of such financial assistance. In addition, H.R. 5175 contains a similar prospective prohibition for those holding or negotiating for Outer Continental Shelf oil and gas leases. S. 3295 and S. 3628 do not contain a similar prohibition.

Foreign Nationals

Several questions of interpretation could be raised by Section 102 of the legislation, which would apply existing prohibitions on contributions or expenditures by foreign nationals to foreign-controlled domestic corporations (e.g., U.S. subsidiaries of foreign corporations). For example, it is unclear how the FEC or a court would interpret or administer some of the key terms contained in the various thresholds for establishing foreign control, as proposed in Section 102. One such threshold focuses upon direct or indirect ownership by a foreign national of various amounts of the voting shares of a corporation (see **Table 1**), but would appear to leave the FEC substantial discretion in determining what constitutes "indirect ownership" or at what point in time ownership is determined. Other criteria similarly focus upon whether one or more foreign nationals "has the power to direct, dictate, or control the decision-making process of the corporation" with respect to its interests in the United States or in connection with its federal, state, or local election activities, including PAC administration and making contributions and expenditures. However, this standard would also appear to leave the FEC substantial discretion to determine what forms of conduct or business arrangements would indicate that a foreign national has the power to "direct, dictate, or control" corporate decision-making.

Coordinated Party Expenditures

Section 104 of the legislation appears to lift the existing caps on coordinated party expenditures unless "the communication is controlled by, or made at the direction of, the candidate or an authorized committee of the candidate."[51] In the absence of increased contribution limits, candidates may face substantial obstacles responding to corporate and union advertising post-*Citizens United.* Lifting the caps on coordinated party expenditures arguably provides parties with a way to help their candidates facing potential corporate, union, or tax-exempt organization-funded advertising. On the other hand, some may object to increasing the amount of money in the political system, even if it is to respond to corporate or union advertising. In addition, the standard for communications "controlled by, or made at the direction of, the candidate or an authorized committee of the candidate" is not defined. Given this potential ambiguity, and an ongoing FEC rulemaking on coordination, some in Congress might wish to clarify terms.

Potential Effects of Disclosure and Disclaimer Provisions

The bills would require additional disclosure of donors to covered organizations. The provisions may be understood, at least in part, as a mechanism to limit the possibility that non-profit organizations might be used as "shadow groups"—groups to which corporations, other entities, or individuals would give funds to be used for campaign activities with little or no public disclosure. A notable aspect of the bills is that they would require the disclosure of certain donors who did not give money specifically for political activities, unlike, for example, the existing independent expenditure provision, which only requires the disclosure of donors who gave "for the purpose of furthering" the expenditure.[52]

Another potentially notable aspect of the donor disclosure provisions is that they would apply FEC reporting requirements to § 527 *political organizations* that are not *political committees* under FECA. These political organizations would include the "§ 527 groups" that have been controversial in recent years because they seem intended to influence federal elections in ways that might be outside the scope of FECA. Under current law, political committees report to the FEC, while the § 527 groups report to the IRS.[53] In both cases, the information is publicly available. The other types of covered organizations are not currently subject to similar reporting requirements.

The bills' disclosure and disclaimer requirements would not necessarily, in and of themselves, limit overall spending on political advertising. Ultimately, corporations, unions, and other groups intent on making independent expenditures and electioneering communications could choose to do so regardless of such requirements. The additional requirements proposed in the bills might, however, cause potential advertisers to consider whether they wish to be publicly accountable for the advertising.

Campaign-Related Activity Accounts

Section 213 of the bills would permit covered organizations to establish optional accounts for campaign-related activity, including independent expenditures and electioneering communications. Because such accounts do not currently exist, it is unclear how significant this provision might be. Several issues, however, could be relevant. First, it appears that once an organization elected to establish the account, it would be required to use that account exclusively for future *campaign-related activity*—a strategic or administrative decision that some organizations might not be willing to make on a permanent basis. Second, the provisions specify that amounts in the account be "exclusively for disbursements by the covered organization for campaign-related activity."[54] Given this language, it is unclear whether or not an organization using a campaign-related activity account could dispose of its funds if it decided to abandon political spending altogether. If Congress wishes to provide a non-campaign-related mechanism to do so, existing provisions in FECA permitting charitable contributions could be an option.[55]

Potential Implementation Concerns

Even if Congress enacts the DISCLOSE Act quickly, aspects of the legislation will require agency implementation. The process could affect how quickly and how clearly the act affects campaigns and related spending (e.g., independent political advertising). Because the DISCLOSE Act would primarily amend FECA, the FEC would be responsible for administering and enforcing most of the bill's provisions.[56]

It is possible that the FEC could implement the DISCLOSE Act quickly, although various factors suggest that it is unlikely the Commission could fully implement the act before the 2010 November general elections.[57] In addition to the time required to develop and reach agreement on rules, for those rules to be finalized (upon publication in the *Federal Register*), the Commission would have to also approve an *explanation and justification* (E&J) statement explaining its rationale and offering practical guidance about what the regulations mean and how they will be enforced. This process routinely takes months, even for expedited rulemakings. The Commission would have to also amend its reporting forms to adhere to the act's new requirements.

Importantly, FECA requires that adopting rules and developing forms (among other provisions) requires affirmative votes from at least four of the six Commissioners.[58] A series of deadlocked votes (e.g., 3-3 ties) among members of the current Commission, however, suggests that disagreement among Commissioners is possible—particularly on controversial or ambiguous aspects of the legislation.[59] If disagreements resulted in deadlock or failure to implement the law as Congress intends, the DISCLOSE Act's effectiveness could be delayed or compromised.

Perhaps in response to those concerns, many of the DISCLOSE Act's provisions would become effective 30 days after enactment, with at least one becoming effective immediately upon enactment. The bills specify that their provisions would generally take effect regardless of whether the FEC had promulgated rules to implement the legislation. Nonetheless, the "regulated community" might lack practical and administrative guidance about how to comply with the act's provisions until the Commission could issue rules and begin considering advisory opinions. Nonetheless, even if rulemaking or amending forms were delayed, the law itself would still take effect as stated in the act. Therefore, even if some details remained to be determined, enacting the DISCLOSE Act or other legislation could permit Congress to place additional requirements on political advertisers or other campaign actors regardless of Commission action or inaction.

CONCLUSION

As Congress considers the DISCLOSE Act, it may be too soon to predict precisely how *Citizens United* might affect campaigns or political advertising in the absence of legislation. If Congress chooses to enact the DISCLOSE Act, it would provide additional information to the public and regulators about political advertising funded by corporations, unions, and tax-exempt organizations. It would also prohibit certain entities from funding electioneering communications and independent expenditures, as well as providing political parties with greater ability to make coordinated party expenditures in some cases.

Except for the spending prohibitions in the bill, nothing in the legislation would necessarily prevent corporations, unions, or other entities from funding political advertising calling for election or defeat of clearly identified candidates. The disclosure and disclaimer provisions could, however, provide the public and regulators with additional information about the sources of that advertising. Public disclosure could also cause would-be advertisers to think carefully before making political expenditures. For those who believe that *Citizens United* will usher in a new era of corporate or union dominance in elections, such an outcome might be welcome. On the other hand, those who believe that *Citizens United* correctly strengthens corporate and union speech ights might be wary of any provisions perceived as stifling the ability to participate in elections. As Congress considers the DISCLOSE Act, issues related to how terms are defined, the kinds of organizations that would be regulated, implementation, and other concerns may be relevant.

ACKNOWLEDGMENTS

Kate M. Manuel, Legislative Attorney, contributed to this report.

Table 1. Comparison of Major Provisions of H.R. 5175, S. 3628, and S. 3295 with Current Federal Law

Major Policy Issue	Overview of Major Relevant Provisions in Current Federal Law	Overview of Major Provisions in H.R. 5175 as Passed by the House	Overview of Major Provisions in S. 3628 as Introduced in the Senate	Overview of Major Provisions in S. 3295 as Introduced in the Senate
Findings		No comparable provision.	Would set forth general and specific findings in support of the legislation. [§ 2]	With some modifications, similar to S. 3628 as introduced in the Senate, (hereinafter "S. 3628"). [§ 2]
Definition of Independent Expenditure	Independent expenditure is defined as an expenditure "expressly advocating the election or defeat of a clearly identified candidate" and that is not made in coordination with a candidate or party. [2 U.S.C. § 431(17)] According to Supreme Court precedent, the "functional equivalent of express advocacy" is a communication that is susceptible of no reasonable interpretation other than as an appeal to vote for or against a specific candidate.	Would expand definition of independent expenditure to include an expenditure "that, when taken as a whole, expressly advocates the election or defeat of a clearly identified candidate, or is the functional equivalent of express advocacy because it can be interpreted by a reasonable person only as advocating the election or defeat of a candidate, taking into account whether the communication involved mentions a candidacy, a political party, or a challenger to a candidate, or takes a position on a candidate's character, qualifications, or fitness for office."	Substantially similar to H.R. 5175 as passed by the House (hereinafter "H.R. 5175"). [§ 201]	Substantially similar to H.R. 5175 and S. 3628. [§ 201]

Table 1. (Continued).

Major Policy Issue	Overview of Major Relevant Provisions in Current Federal Law	Overview of Major Provisions in H.R. 5175 as Passed by the House	Overview of Major Provisions in S. 3628 as Introduced in the Senate	Overview of Major Provisions in S. 3295 as Introduced in the Senate
	[Citizens United v. FEC, 130 S. Ct. 876, 889-90 (2010), quoting FEC v. Wisconsin Right to Life, Inc., 551 U.S. 449, 469-70 (2007)]	Would impose 24-hour reporting requirement for expenditures of $10,000 or more made during the period up to and including the 20th day before an election and expenditures of $1,000 or more made during the period after the 20th day, but more than 24 hours before an election. [§ 201]		
Definition of Electioneering Major Policy Issue Communication	Electioneering communication is Overview of Major Relevant Provisions in Current Federal Law defined as a broadcast, cable, or satellite transmission that refers to a clearly identified federal office candidate and is made within 60 days of a general election (or within 30 days of a primary). [2 U.S.C. § 434(f)(3)(A)(i)(II)]	Would expand period prior to Overview of Major Provisions in H.R. 5175 as Passed by the House general election in which communications are treated as electioneering communications to 120 days. [§ 202]	Substantially similar to H.R. 5175. Overview of Major Provisions in S. 3628 as Introduced in the Senate [§ 202]	Would expand period prior to Overview of Major Provisions in S. 3295 as Introduced in the Senate general election in which communications are treated as electioneering communications to 90 days. [§ 202]

Major Policy Issue	Overview of Major Relevant Provisions in Current Federal Law	Overview of Major Provisions in H.R. 5175 as Passed by the House	Overview of Major Provisions in S. 3628 as Introduced in the Senate	Overview of Major Provisions in S. 3295 as Introduced in the Senate
Definition of Public Communication Exempting Free Internet Communications	Public Communication is defined as a communication by means of broadcast, cable, or satellite communication, newspaper, magazine, outdoor advertising facility, mass mailing, or telephone bank to the general public, or any other form of general public political advertising. [2 U.S.C. § 431(22)]	Would exempt Internet communications, unless placed for a fee on another person's website, from being treated as a form of "general public political advertising," thereby exempting such communications from the definition of public communication. [§ 105]	Substantially similar to H.R. 5175. [§ 105]	No relevant provision.
Involvement in Federal Elections by Foreign Nationals	Foreign nationals are prohibited from making contributions in federal, state, or local elections, and are prohibited from making independent expenditures and electioneering communications in federal elections, [2 U.S.C. § 441e], but U.S. subsidiaries of foreign corporations may form PACs to make expenditures and contributions under certain circumstances. FEC regulations provide that foreign nationals shall not "direct, dictate, control, or directly or indirectly participate" in the decision-making process of a corporation, labor union, political committee, or political organization with regard to	Would expand the definition of foreign national to prohibit contributions in federal, state, or local elections; and independent expenditures and electioneering communications in federal elections by foreign-controlled domestic corporations as follows: (1) if the foreign national is a foreign country, foreign government official, or a corporation principally owned or controlled by a foreign government or official, and the foreign national directly or indirectly owns or controls at least 5% of the corporation's voting shares; or (2) if the foreign national is other than a foreign country, foreign	Substantially similar to H.R. 5175. [§ 102]	Would expand the definition of foreign national to prohibit contributions in federal, state, or local elections; and independent expenditures and electioneering communications in federal elections by foreign-controlled domestic corporations as follows: (1) if a foreign national directly or indirectly owns at least 20% of the corporation's voting shares; or (2) if a majority of the corporation's board members are foreign nationals; or (3) if one or more foreign national can "direct, dictate, or control" the corporation's decision-making process with respect to its U.S. interests; or

Table 1. (Continued).

Major Policy Issue	Overview of Major Relevant Provisions in Current Federal Law	Overview of Major Provisions in H.R. 5175 as Passed by the House	Overview of Major Provisions in S. 3628 as Introduced in the Senate	Overview of Major Provisions in S. 3295 as Introduced in the Senate
	federal or non-federal election-related activities, such as decisions concerning the making of contributions, donations, expenditures, or disbursements in connection with federal, state or local election or regarding the administration of a political committee. [11 C.F.R. § 110.20(i)]	government official, or a corporation principally owned or controlled by a foreign government or official, and the foreign national directly or indirectly owns or controls at least 20% of the corporation's voting shares; or (3) if at least two foreign nationals, each of whom owns or controls at least 5% of the corporation's voting shares, directly or indirectly own or control at least 50% of the corporation's voting shares; or (4) if a majority of the corporation's board members are foreign nationals; (5) if one or more foreign nationals can "direct, dictate, or control" the corporations' decision-making process with respect to its U.S. interests; or (6) if one or more foreign nationals can "direct, dictate, or control" decision-making of the corporation with respect to its activities in connection with federal, state, or local elections, including making contributions, donations, expenditures, independent expenditures, disbursements for electioneering communications or administration of a PAC established or maintained by the corporation. [§ 102]		(4) if one or more foreign nationals can "direct, dictate, or control" decision-making of the corporation with respect to its activities in connection with federal, state, or local elections, including making contributions, donations, expenditures, independent expenditures, disbursements for electioneering communications or administration of a PAC established or maintained by the corporation. [§ 102]

Table 1. (Continued).

Major Policy Issue	Overview of Major Relevant Provisions in Current Federal Law	Overview of Major Provisions in H.R. 5175 as Passed by the House	Overview of Major Provisions in S. 3628 as Introduced in the Senate	Overview of Major Provisions in S. 3295 as Introduced in the Senate
Major Policy Issue	Overview of Major Relevant Provisions in Current Federal Law	Overview of Major Provisions in H.R. 5175 as Passed by the House	Overview of Major Provisions in S. 3628 as Introduced in the Senate	Overview of Major Provisions in S. 3295 as Introduced in the Senate
		Would require CEOs (or highest-ranking corporate official) to certify under penalty of perjury, to the FEC, before making expenditures in connection with federal office elections, that the foreign-national prohibitions above do not apply to the corporation. [§ 102] Would clarify that provision does not prohibit a corporation which is not a foreign national from establishing a political action committee (PAC), or from making a lawful contribution in a state or local election, so long as none of the funds in the PAC or as used for the state-contribution are provided by a foreign national and no foreign national has power to "direct, dictate, or control" the PAC or state-level contribution. [§ 102]	Substantially similar to H.R. 5175 [§ 102]	

Table 1. (Continued).

Major Policy Issue	Overview of Major Relevant Provisions in Current Federal Law	Overview of Major Provisions in H.R. 5175 as Passed by the House	Overview of Major Provisions in S. 3628 as Introduced in the Senate	Overview of Major Provisions in S. 3295 as Introduced in the Senate
Involvement in Federal Elections by Government Contractors	Government contractors are prohibited from making contributions. [2 U.S.C. § 441c]	Would prohibit government contractors holding contracts of $10 million or more from making independent expenditures and electioneering communications. [§ 101]	Substantially similar to H.R. 5175. [§ 101]	Would prohibit government contractors holding contracts of $50,000 or more from making independent expenditures and electioneering communications. [§ 101]
Contributions, Independent Expenditures, and Electioneering Communications by Those Receiving TARP Funds	Corporations are prohibited from using general treasury funds to make contributions. [2 U.S.C. § 441b(a)] As a result of Citizens United, it appears that regardless of whether having received TARP funds, corporations are permitted to use general treasury funds to make independent expenditures and electioneering communications. [Citizens United v. FEC, 130 S. Ct. 876 (2010)]	Would prohibit entities receiving or negotiating for TARP funds from making contributions, independent expenditures, or electioneering communications until the funds were repaid (or if the negotiations ended without the entity receiving funds). Prohibition would begin on the later of the commencement of the negotiations for such financial assistance under title I of the Emergency Economic Stabilization Act of 2008 or the date of enactment H.R. 5175, and end on the later of the ending of negotiations or the repayment of such financial assistance. [§ 101]	Substantially similar to H.R. 5175 and S. 3295. [§ 101]	Substantially similar to H.R. 5175 and S. 3628. [§ 101]

Major Policy Issue	Overview of Major Relevant Provisions in Current Federal Law	Overview of Major Provisions in H.R. 5175 as Passed by the House	Overview of Major Provisions in S. 3628 as Introduced in the Senate	Overview of Major Provisions in S. 3295 as Introduced in the Senate
Contributions, Independent Expenditures, and Electioneering Communications by Those Holding and Negotiating Outer Continental Shelf Oil and Gas Leases	No existing prohibition specifically on those holding oil and gas leases. Corporations are prohibited from using general treasury funds to make contributions. [2 U.S.C. § 441b(a)] As a result of Citizens United, corporations are permitted to use general treasury funds to make independent expenditures and electioneering communications. [Citizens United v. FEC, 130 S. Ct. 876 (2010)]	Would prohibit those holding or negotiating for Outer Continental Shelf oil and gas leases from making contributions, independent expenditures, and electioneering communications. Prohibition would begin on the later of the commencement of the lease negotiations or the date of enactment of H.R. 5175, and end on the later of the ending of negotiations or termination of the lease. [§ 101]	No relevant provision.	No relevant provision.
Definition of Covered Organization for Purposes of the Act's Disclosure and Disclaimer Provisions	Not relevant under current law. IRC § 501(c) describes entities that qualify for tax-exempt status, including § 501(c)(3) charitable organizations; § 501(c)(4) social welfare organizations; § 501(c)(5)	Would define covered organizations as corporations, labor unions, § 501(c)(4), (c)(5), and (c)(6) organizations, and § 527 political organizations that are not political committees under FECA.	Substantially similar to H.R. 5175. [§ 211(a), (b), (c); § 212; § 213; § 214; § 301; exception for qualifying § 501(c)(4) organizations is in § 211(c)]	Substantially similar to H.R. 5175 and S. 3628, but no exclusion for § 501(c)(3) organizations and qualifying § 501(c)(4) organizations. [§ 212]

Table 1. (Continued).

Major Policy Issue	Overview of Major Relevant Provisions in Current Federal Law	Overview of Major Provisions in H.R. 5175 as Passed by the House	Overview of Major Provisions in S. 3628 as Introduced in the Senate	Overview of Major Provisions in S. 3295 as Introduced in the Senate
	labor unions, and § 501(c)(6) trade associations. Many	Would expressly exclude § 501(c)(3) organizations from the		
	organizations are incorporated. § 501(c)(4), (c)(5), and (c)(6) organizations may engage in a limited amount of campaign activity under the IRC, although there may be tax consequences.a § 501(c)(3) organizations are absolutely prohibited from engaging in such activity. What is campaign activity under the IRC and FECA might not always be the same. IRC § 527 provides tax-exempt status to political organizations with the primary purpose of influencing elections or engaging in similar activities. Under FECA, political committees are entities receiving contributions or making expenditures aggregating at least $1,000 per year for the purpose of influencing federal elections.	definition. Also excluded would be § 501(c)(4) organizations that do not use funds from corporations or labor unions for campaign-related activity if the organization had § 501(c)(4) status for at least 10 years; had at least 500,000 dues-paying members who were individuals and at least one member in each state, D.C., and Puerto Rico during the prior year; and received no more than 15% of total donations from corporations or labor unions during the prior year. [§ 211(a), (b), (c); § 212; § 213; § 214; § 301; exception for qualifying § 501(c)(4) organizations is in § 211(c)]		

Major Policy Issue	Overview of Major Relevant Provisions in Current Federal Law	Overview of Major Provisions in H.R. 5175 as Passed by the House	Overview of Major Provisions in S. 3628 as Introduced in the Senate	Overview of Major Provisions in S. 3295 as Introduced in the Senate
Major Policy Issue	Overview of Major Relevant Provisions in Current Federal Law	Overview of Major Provisions in H.R. 5175 as Passed by the House	Overview of Major Provisions in S. 3628 as Introduced in the Senate	Overview of Major Provisions in S. 3295 as Introduced in the Senate
	The term political organization is broader than political committee, in part because it includes groups intending to influence state and local elections and the groups colloquially referred to as 527s that have been controversial in recent years because they appear intended to influence federal elections in ways that may place them outside the definition of political committee. [IRC §§ 501(c), 527; 2 U.S.C. § 431(4)(A), (8)(A), (9)(A)]			
Stand by Your Ad Disclaimers in Political Advertising	Corporations and labor unions funding express advocacy messages are required to indentify in the communication: their name, address, and contact information; and that the communication "is not authorized by any candidate or candidate's committee." [2 U.S.C. § 441d(a)(3)]	Would expand types of communications funded by "covered organizations" that trigger disclaimer requirements to include disbursements for an "independent expenditure consisting of a public communication." [§ 214]	Substantially similar to H.R. 5175. [§ 214]	Substantially similar to H.R. 5175 and S. 3628. [§ 214]

Table 1. (Continued).

Major Policy Issue	Overview of Major Relevant Provisions in Current Federal Law	Overview of Major Provisions in H.R. 5175 as Passed by the House	Overview of Major Provisions in S. 3628 as Introduced in the Senate	Overview of Major Provisions in S. 3295 as Introduced in the Senate
	Corporate and union radio and TV ads are required to include an audio statement that the corporation or union paid for the ad. In TV ads, the statement is required to be conveyed by a view or voice-over of a corporate or union representative. [2 U.S.C. § 441d(d)(2)]	Would expand disclaimer requirements for disbursements by covered organizations for independent expenditures or electioneering communications to require the organization's CEO or highest ranking official or any "significant funder" to state their approval for the communication, and would require listing the "Top Five Funders." [§ 214]	Substantially similar to H.R. 5175. [§ 214]	Substantially similar to H.R. 5175 and S. 3628. [§ 214]
	Candidates are currently required to state their approval for their broadcast advertising. [2 U.S.C. § 441d(d)(1)]	Would require disclaimers to include name of person approving message and name of any "significant funder" (if the communication is an independent expenditure consisting of a public communication and is paid in whole or in part with disbursement by covered organization for campaign-related activity), and the local jurisdiction and state where individual resides or organization's principal office is located. [§ 214]	Substantially similar to H.R. 5175, except it would not require the disclaimers to include the local jurisdiction and state where the individual resides or the organization's principal office location, but would require that the title of the individual approving the message be provided. [§ 214]	Substantially similar to H.R. 5175 and S. 3628, except that it would not require the disclaimers to include the local jurisdiction and state where the individual resides or the organization's principal office is located, nor would it require that the title of the individual approving the message be provided. [§ 214]

Major Policy Issue	Overview of Major Relevant Provisions in Current Federal Law	Overview of Major Provisions in H.R. 5175 as Passed by the House	Overview of Major Provisions in S. 3628 as Introduced in the Senate	Overview of Major Provisions in S. 3295 as Introduced in the Senate
		Would provide exemption to disclaimer requirements if on the basis of criteria established in FEC regulations, the communication is so short that including disclaimer would constitute a hardship. [§ 214] Would expand application of disclaimer requirements to cover political committees that accept contributions or donations that do not comply with FECA contribution limits or source prohibitions. [§ 214]	Substantially similar. [§ 214] No relevant provision.	Substantially similar. [§ 214] No relevant provision
Disclaimers for Automated Political Telephone Calls (Robo Calls)	Election law and telecommunications law do not address political robo calls per se. Robo calls that advocate for election or defeat of candidates or solicit funds appear to require disclaimers stating who paid for the communication. [2 U.S.C. § 441d(a)] Among other requirements, telecommunications law appears to require that prerecorded phone calls identify the entity responsible for the call at the beginning of the message [47 U.S.C. § 227(d)(3); 47 C.F.R. § 64.1200(b)(2)].	Would require political robo calls to include a disclaimer. Would also require disclosure of top five funders for an electioneering communication or independent expenditure consisting of a public communication made or paid for by covered organizations or political committees that accept contributions or donations that do not comply with FECA contribution limits or source prohibitions. Both disclosure and disclaimer would have to be made at the beginning of the call, unless the FEC determined that the message was so short that doing so would be a hardship. [§ 214]	Substantially similar to H.R. 5175 [§ 214]	No relevant provision.

Table 1. (Continued).

Major Policy Issue	Overview of Major Relevant Provisions in Current Federal Law	Overview of Major Provisions in H.R. 5175 as Passed by the House	Overview of Major Provisions in S. 3628 as Introduced in the Senate	Overview of Major Provisions in S. 3295 as Introduced in the Senate
Disclosure of Expenditures Disclosure of donors to covered organizations making independent expenditures and electioneering communications	In quarterly reports to the FEC, entities making independent expenditures in excess of $250 during a calendar year must disclose donors who contribute more than $200 "for the purpose of furthering" the expenditure. If the entity spends at least $10,000 toward independent expenditures during an election year, those expenditures must be reported to the FEC within 48 hours if the expenditure occurred up to 20 days before the general election. Entities that spend at least $1,000 on independent expenditures less than 20 days before the election must report that spending to the FEC within 24 hours. Donors of more than $200 must also be included in the 48-hour and 24-hour reports. [2 U.S.C. § 434(c)(2)(C); 11 C.F.R. § 109.10]	Would require covered organizations making public independent expenditures that aggregate at least $10,000 in a calendar year to disclose, within 48 hours: (1) donors who gave at least $600 for campaign-related activity or in response to solicitation for funds for such activity (along with the candidate, election, or public independent expenditure, if specified by donor); and (2) donors who gave unrestricted donations during the reporting period of at least: - $6,000 if the disbursements were made exclusively from a Campaign-Related Activity Account (CRAA) and the organization made deposits of at least $10,000 into account during reporting period, or	Substantially similar to H.R. 5175. [§ 211(a),(b)]	Substantially similar to H.R. 5175 and S. 3628; except that the reporting thresholds for donors of independent expenditures would be $1,000 and $10,000; no higher donor-disclosure threshold for organizations deemed to have made a transfer; and all electioneering communications would have to be made from CRAA in order to qualify for higher donor-disclosure threshold. [§ 211(a), (b)].

Major Policy Issue	Overview of Major Relevant Provisions in Current Federal Law	Overview of Major Provisions in H.R. 5175 as Passed by the House	Overview of Major Provisions in S. 3628 as Introduced in the Senate	Overview of Major Provisions in S. 3295 as Introduced in the Senate
	Entities making at least $10,000 in electioneering communications must disclose donors who contribute at least $1,000; however, if the disbursement is made from a separate account that contains only contributions by U.S. citizens and legal resident aliens made directly to the account for electioneering communications, then only those donors who contribute at least $1,000 to the account are disclosed. [2 U.S.C. § 434(f)(2)(E), (F)] 11 C.F.R. § 104.20 contains rules for corporations, labor unions, and qualified nonprofit corporations that make certain types of electioneering communications. Its applicability in light of Citizens United is unclear.	- $600 if any disbursement was not from the CRAA. If organization is deemed to have made a transfer (see below), thresholds would be increased to $10,000. Rules essentially the same for covered organizations making at least $10,000 in electioneering communications, although the $600 and $6,000 amounts are increased to $1,000 and $10,000. To get benefit of higher threshold, organization must make from the CRAA those electioneering communications that it reasonably believes are for a § 527 exempt function.a Donor-disclosure rules would not apply to payments received in the regular course of business. [§ 211(a), (b)]		

Table 1. (Continued).

Major Policy Issue	Overview of Major Relevant Provisions in Current Federal Law	Overview of Major Provisions in H.R. 5175 as Passed by the House	Overview of Major Provisions in S. 3628 as Introduced in the Senate	Overview of Major Provisions in S. 3295 as Introduced in the Senate
	Section 527 political organizations that are not political committees under FECA are generally required to periodically report information regarding their donors and expenditures to the IRS (or a state). Such information is made publically available. The reporting requirement does not apply to expenditures that are independent expenditures. [26 U.S.C. § 527(j), (k)]	If organization uses CRAA, all disbursements for campaign-related activity would have to come from CRAA except for those which the organization reasonably believes would not be treated as for a § 527 exempt function,a and account funds would have to be used "exclusively" for such purposes.	Substantially similar to H.R. 5175. [§ 213]	Substantially similar to H.R. 5175 and S. 3628, except no exclusion for disbursements not treated as made for a § 527 exempt function; a no express language addressing treatment of accounts for purposes of IRC § 527(f)(3);a and CRAA could not contain funds that donor notified organization in writing could not be used for such activity. [§ 213]

Major Policy Issue	Overview of Major Relevant Provisions in Current Federal Law	Overview of Major Provisions in H.R. 5175 as Passed by the House	Overview of Major Provisions in S. 3628 as Introduced in the Senate	Overview of Major Provisions in S. 3295 as Introduced in the Senate
		CRAA would contain: donations made for campaign-related activity or in response to solicitations for funds for such activity; and amounts transferred from other accounts (including general treasury funds). Could not contain funds which the organization and donor "mutually agreed" would not be used for such activity. The establishment or administration of the CRAA would not, by itself, be treated as the establishment or administration of a political committee. Nonetheless, it "may" be treated as a separate segregated fund for purposes of IRC § 527(f)(3).a [§ 213] If the donation would be disclosed and the organization and donor "mutually agree" at the time of the donation that the funds are not to be used for campaign-related activity, then the organization's CFO would have to certify to the donor, within 30 days of receipt, that the funds would not be used for such activity and the person's identity would not be disclosed through the bill's disclosure or disclaimer provisions. [§ 212]		

Table 1. (Continued).

Major Policy Issue	Overview of Major Relevant Provisions in Current Federal Law	Overview of Major Provisions in H.R. 5175 as Passed by the House	Overview of Major Provisions in S. 3628 as Introduced in the Senate	Overview of Major Provisions in S. 3295 as Introduced in the Senate
		An organization only subject to reporting requirements because it was deemed to have made a transfer (see below) would not have to file report if all donors were individuals and any donor making a donation for campaign-related activity or unrestricted donation during the reporting period gave less than $10,000. [§ 211(a),(b)]	Substantially similar to H.R. 5175. [§ 212] Substantially similar to H.R. 5175. [§ 211(a),(b)]	If donor notified organization in writing that the funds were not to be used for campaign-related activity, then the organization's CFO would have to certify to the donor within seven days of receipt that the funds would not be used for such activity and the person's identity would not be disclosed through the bill's disclosure or disclaimer provisions. [§ 212] No comparable provision.
Disclosure of Expenditures	No comparable existing statutory provision.	A covered organization would be treated as making a public independent expenditure or	Substantially similar to H.R. 5175.	Substantially similar to H.R. 5175 and S. 3628.
Transfers subsequently used for campaign activity		electioneering communication if it transferred funds to another person for such purpose or was deemed to have made a transfer. The organization would be deemed to have made such a transfer if:	Substantially similar to H.R. 5175.	The organization would be deemed to have made such a transfer if:

Major Policy Issue	Overview of Major Relevant Provisions in Current Federal Law	Overview of Major Provisions in H.R. 5175 as Passed by the House	Overview of Major Provisions in S. 3628 as Introduced in the Senate	Overview of Major Provisions in S. 3295 as Introduced in the Senate
		• it designates, requests, or suggests that the amounts be used for public independent expenditures or electioneering communications and the transferee agrees to do so; • the person making the expenditure (or someone acting on his/her behalf) expressly solicited the organization for funds for making or paying for such expenditures; • it and the transferee engaged in written or oral discussions regarding the transferee making or paying for such expenditures (or donating or transferring the amounts to another person for such purpose); • it knew or had reason to know that the transferee intended to make such expenditures; or		• the person making the expenditure (or someone acting on his/her behalf) solicited funds from the transferor or transferee for making such expenditures; • there were "substantial discussions" about such expenditures between the transferor and transferee; • the transferor or transferee knew (or should have known) of the covered organization's intent to make such expenditures; or • the transferor or transferee made a public independent expenditure or electioneering communication in the current or previous election cycle.

Table 1. (Continued).

Major Policy Issue	Overview of Major Relevant Provisions in Current Federal Law	Overview of Major Provisions in H.R. 5175 as Passed by the House	Overview of Major Provisions in S. 3628 as Introduced in the Senate	Overview of Major Provisions in S. 3295 as Introduced in the Senate
		• it or the transferee made at least $50,000 in public independent expenditures or electioneering communications during the two-year period ending on the date of the transfer. An exception would exist for commercial transactions occurring in the ordinary course of business between the organization and transferee (unless there was affirmative evidence that the amounts were transferred for the purpose of making such expenditures), or the covered organization and transferee mutually agreed that the funds would not be used for campaign-related activity. Exception would also exist for transfers between affiliated organizations (including § 501(c)(3) organizations) if the aggregate amount transferred during the year was less than $50,000 and neither organization was established for the purpose of disbursing funds for campaign-related activity.		

		For determining whether the $50,000 threshold was met, funds attributable to dues, fees, or assessments paid by individuals on a regular, periodic basis in accordance with a per-individual calculation that was made on a regular basis would be attributed to the individual and not the organization. An organization would be an affiliate of another if its governing instrument required it to be bound the other's decisions; it is charted by the other organization; or its governing board includes designated representatives of the other organization or includes persons who have a certain relationship to the other organization or whose service on the board is contingent upon the other organization's approval. [§ 211(a),(b)]	Substantially similar to H.R. 5175. Exception would also exist for transfers between affiliated organizations. If the transfer[s] aggregated at least $50,000 during the year, then the report filed by the transferee organization must include the information required relating to donations and payments made to the affiliate which transferred the funds and to any affiliate which transferred at least $50,000 in the 12-month period prior to the transfer.	An exception would exist for commercial transactions occurring in the ordinary course of business. Additionally, funds may not be used for campaign-related activity if the donor notifies the organization in writing that the funds may not be used for such purpose. No comparable provision. [§ 211(a),(b); § 212]

Table 1. (Continued).

Major Policy Issue	Overview of Major Relevant Provisions in Current Federal Law	Overview of Major Provisions in H.R. 5175 as Passed by the House	Overview of Major Provisions in S. 3628 as Introduced in the Senate	Overview of Major Provisions in S. 3295 as Introduced in the Senate
			Affiliates would be a membership organization and its related state and local entities; a national or international labor organization and its local union, or an organization of national or international unions and its state and local central bodies; and a corporation and its wholly owned subsidiaries. [§ 211(a),(b)]	
CEO Certification of Certain Information to the FEC	No comparable existing statutory provision.	If a covered organization makes a disbursement for "campaign-related activity" during the calendar quarter, the CEO or designee would be required to certify to FEC, within 15 days of the quarter's end, that the disbursement was made in compliance with applicable law. [§ 212] (See also CEO certification requirements in the Involvement in Federal Elections by Foreign Nationals row above. [§ 102])	Substantially similar to H.R. 5175 and S. 3295. [§ 212]	Substantially similar to H.R. 5175 and S. 3628. [§ 212]
Indexing for Inflation	FECA currently contains some indexing provisions (e.g., 2 U.S.C. § 441a(c)) but they are generally inapplicable to the relevant new provisions in the DISCLOSE Act.	Would index various reporting thresholds (e.g., for donor disclosure) established in the bill. [§ 215]	Substantially similar to H.R. 5175 [§ 215]	No comparable provision.

Major Policy Issue	Overview of Major Relevant Provisions in Current Federal Law	Overview of Major Provisions in H.R. 5175 as Passed by the House	Overview of Major Provisions in S. 3628 as Introduced in the Senate	Overview of Major Provisions in S. 3295 as Introduced in the Senate
Disclosure of Certain Lobbyist Spending	Lobbyists must semiannually report "contributions" exceeding $200 made to candidates, leadership PACs, or parties. [2 U.S.C. § 1604(d)(1)(D)] (Note: Additional FEC electioneering communication and independent expenditure reporting requirements may apply to lobbyists in certain circumstances, but are not intended to apply specifically to lobbyists.)	Would require lobbyists to disclose in certain Lobbying Disclosure Act (LDA) reports: (1) independent expenditures of at least $1,000 funded by those lobbyists; the names of candidates supported or opposed in the ads; and the amount spent supporting or opposing each candidate; (2) electioneering communications of at least $1,000 funded by lobbyists; the names of candidates referred to in the ads. [§ 221]	Substantially similar to H.R. 5175; however in addition to disclosure of electioneering communications of at least $1,000 funded by lobbyists, and the names of candidates referred to in the ads, would also require disclosure of whether the ad supported or opposed the candidate. [§ 221]	Substantially similar to H.R. 5175 and S. 3628. [§ 221]
Disclosure to Shareholders, Members, and Donors of Covered Organizations	There is no comparable requirement, although disclosure may be required to the FEC (e.g., for independent expenditures or electioneering communications) or, in the case of tax-exempt organizations, to the IRS, and such information is generally subject to public disclosure. [2 U.S.C. § 434; 26 U.S.C. §§ 527, 6033, 6103]	Would require a covered organization to disclose disbursements for campaign-related activity in any "regular, periodic reports" on its finances/activities provided to its shareholders, members, and donors.	Substantially similar to H.R. 5175. [§ 301]	Substantially similar information must be reported as under H.R. 5175 and S. 3628, although no requirement it be reported in a "clear and conspicuous manner."

Table 1. (Continued).

Major Policy Issue	Overview of Major Relevant Provisions in Current Federal Law	Overview of Major Provisions in H.R. 5175 as Passed by the House	Overview of Major Provisions in S. 3628 as Introduced in the Senate	Overview of Major Provisions in S. 3295 as Introduced in the Senate
		Information would include the date and amount spent, the source of the funds, the name of candidates referred to in the ads and whether the ads supported or opposed the candidate, and information about transferred funds. The information would have to be reported in a "clear and conspicuous manner." A covered organization would also be required to post a hyperlink on its homepage to the location at the FEC website containing the organizations' reports. The hyperlink would have to be posted within 24 hours after the FEC posts the information and remain on the organization's website for one year following the election. [§ 301]		Within 24 hours of filing reports with FEC, organization would have to post information regarding independent expenditures and electioneering communications on its website, through a direct link from its homepage, in a machine-readable, searchable, sortable, and downloadable manner. Information would have to remain on website for one year following the election. Organization would also have to post a breakdown of disbursements by political party and incumbents/challengers by January 31 in the year following the election and keep the information on the website until the end of that year. [§ 301]

Major Policy Issue	Overview of Major Relevant Provisions in Current Federal Law	Overview of Major Provisions in H.R. 5175 as Passed by the House	Overview of Major Provisions in S. 3628 as Introduced in the Senate	Overview of Major Provisions in S. 3295 as Introduced in the Senate
Coordination of Certain Expenditures	A communication is coordinated (and therefore an in-kind contribution to a candidate or party, or a coordinated party expenditure) with a candidate or a party when the communication satisfies at least one "content" standard and at least one "conduct" standard. A content standard is met, in part, for House or Senate elections, if the communication refers to a candidate and is disseminated within 90 days before the general or primary election, and for presidential and vice presidential elections, if the communication refers to a candidate and is disseminated within 120 days before the primary or nominating convention or caucus.	Would define coordination as a "covered communication," (which "refers" to a candidate and is publically distributed) that is made "in cooperation, consultation, or concert with, or at the request or suggestion of" a candidate or party or any communication that "republishes, disseminates, or distributes" any candidate campaign material. Would exempt from definition of "coordinated communication" communications appearing in a news story, commentary, or editorial distributed through broadcast, newspaper, or magazine, (unless controlled by party, political committee, or candidate) or a candidate debate or forum.	Substantially similar to H.R. 5175. [§ 103]	Substantially similar to H.R. 5175 and S. 3628, although exemption for a news story, commentary, or editorial distributed through broadcast, newspaper, or magazine, (unless controlled by party, political committee, or candidate) or a candidate debate or forum would only apply to "covered communications." [§ 103]
	[11 C.F.R. § 109.21(a),(c)] A conduct standard is met, in part, if the communication is created, produced, or distributed at the request or suggestion of a candidate or party, or at the suggestion of the person paying for the communication and the candidate or party assents to the suggestion, or the communication is created, produced, or distributed after one or more "substantial discussions"	[§ 103]		

Table 1. (Continued).

Major Policy Issue	Overview of Major Relevant Provisions in Current Federal Law	Overview of Major Provisions in H.R. 5175 as Passed by the House	Overview of Major Provisions in S. 3628 as Introduced in the Senate	Overview of Major Provisions in S. 3295 as Introduced in the Senate
	about the communication between the person paying for it and the candidate or party. A discussion is "substantial" if information about the candidate's or party's campaign plan, projects, activities, or needs is conveyed to a person paying for the communication and that information is material to the creation, production, or distribution of the communication. [11 C.F.R. § 109.21(d)]			
		Would expand time period that a communication is considered coordinated between a corporation or union and a House or Senate candidate who is referenced in corporate/union communication, to those made 90 days before the primary through the general election. [§ 103]	Substantially similar to H.R. 5175. [§ 103]	Substantially similar to H.R. 5175 and S. 3628. [§ 103]

Major Policy Issue	Overview of Major Relevant Provisions in Current Federal Law	Overview of Major Provisions in H.R. 5175 as Passed by the House	Overview of Major Provisions in S. 3628 as Introduced in the Senate	Overview of Major Provisions in S. 3295 as Introduced in the Senate
		Would expand time period that coordination is prohibited between corporation or union and presidential or vice presidential candidates, referenced in corporate/union ads made 120 days before the first presidential primary through the general election. [§ 103]	Substantially similar to H.R. 5175. [§ 103]	Substantially similar to H.R. 5175 and S. 3628. [§ 103]
		Would specify that a covered communication may not be considered coordinated "solely on the grounds" that a person "engaged in discussions with the candidate or committee" regarding that person's position on a legislative or policy matter (including urging the candidate or party to adopt that person's position), so long as there is no discussion between the person and the candidate or committee regarding the candidate's campaign plans, projects, activities, or needs. [§ 103]	Substantially similar to H.R. 5175. [§ 103]	No comparable provision.

Table 1. (Continued).

Major Policy Issue	Overview of Major Relevant Provisions in Current Federal Law	Overview of Major Provisions in H.R. 5175 as Passed by the House	Overview of Major Provisions in S. 3628 as Introduced in the Senate	Overview of Major Provisions in S. 3295 as Introduced in the Senate
	Safe Harbor for Endorsements/Solicitations: Provides that a public communication in which a federal office candidate endorses another federal or non-federal candidate is not considered coordinated with respect to the endorsement of the federal candidate unless the public communication promotes, supports, attacks, or opposes the endorsing candidate or another candidate seeking election to the same office. Further provides that a public communication in which a federal office candidate solicits funds for another federal or non-federal candidate, political committee, or tax-exempt organization is not considered coordinated with respect to the soliciting federal office candidate unless the public communication promotes, supports, attacks, or opposes the soliciting candidate or another candidate seeking election to the same office. Safe Harbor for Firewalls:	Would expressly preserve FEC regulations, 11 C.F.R. § 109.21(g) or (h), providing safe harbor for endorsements and solicitations by federal candidates and for establishment and use of a firewall. [§ 103]	Substantially similar to H.R. 5175. [§ 103]	No comparable provision.

Major Policy Issue	Overview of Major Relevant Provisions in Current Federal Law	Overview of Major Provisions in H.R. 5175 as Passed by the House	Overview of Major Provisions in S. 3628 as Introduced in the Senate	Overview of Major Provisions in S. 3295 as Introduced in the Senate
	Provides that "conduct standard," under which coordination is found, is not met if commercial vendor, former employee, or political committee has established a firewall that meets certain requirements. Safe harbor provision does not apply if specific information indicates that despite firewall, information regarding candidate or party campaign plans, projects, activities, or needs, which are material to the creation, production, or distribution of the communication, was used or conveyed to the person paying for the communication. Further provides that firewall must prohibit flow of information between employees or consultants providing services for the person paying for the communication and those employees or consultants providing services to the candidate, who is clearly identified in the communication, or the candidate's opponent, or a party; and that the firewall must be			

Table 1. (Continued).

Major Policy Issue	Overview of Major Relevant Provisions in Current Federal Law	Overview of Major Provisions in H.R. 5175 as Passed by the House	Overview of Major Provisions in S. 3628 as Introduced in the Senate	Overview of Major Provisions in S. 3295 as Introduced in the Senate
	described in a written policy that is distributed to all relevant employees, consultants, and [11 C.F.R. § 109.21 (g), (h)]			
Coordinated Party Expenditure Limits	Provides limits on expenditures by parties in connection with federal office candidates. [2 U.S.C. § 441a(d)]	Would provide that direct costs incurred by a political party for a communication made in connection with a federal office campaign is not subject to the coordinated party expenditure limits unless the communication is "controlled by, or made at the direction of" the candidate or the candidate's authorized committee. [§ 104]	Substantially similar to H.R. 5175. [§ 104]	Substantially similar to H.R. 5175 and S. 3628. [§ 104]
Electronic Filing of Senate Campaign Finance Reports	Senate political committees file campaign finance reports on paper with the Secretary of the Senate. [2 U.S.C. § 432(g)]	No relevant provision.	Would require Senate political committees to electronically file campaign finance reports directly with the FEC. [§ 231]	Substantially similar to S. 3628. [§ 231]
Equal Opportunities Requirement and Reasonable Access Rule	If a broadcaster grants broadcasting time to a candidate for any public office, the broadcaster is required to afford equal opportunities to all other candidates for that same office, with certain exceptions. [47 U.S.C. § 315(a)]	Does not amend current law.	Does not amend current law.	Would expand the equal opportunities requirement to include political parties (in addition to candidates). [§ 401]

Major Policy Issue	Overview of Major Relevant Provisions in Current Federal Law	Overview of Major Provisions in H.R. 5175 as Passed by the House	Overview of Major Provisions in S. 3628 as Introduced in the Senate	Overview of Major Provisions in S. 3295 as Introduced in the Senate
	Broadcasters are required to provide federal office candidates with reasonable access to broadcast stations or permit them to purchase reasonable amounts of broadcast time. [47 U.S.C. 312(a)(7)]	Does not amend current law.	Does not amend current law.	Would expand the reasonable access rule to include reasonable amounts of time purchased at the lowest unit charge (LUC, see below) and makes rule applicable to parties (in addition to candidates). [§ 401]
Lowest Unit Charge (LUC, also Lowest Unit Rate) Provisions	During the 45 days preceding a primary election or 60 days preceding a general election, candidate committees may purchase preemptible broadcast-advertising time at the lowest unit charge (LUC) applicable to a commercial advertiser for comparable time. [47 U.S.C. § 315(b)]	Does not amend current law.	Does not amend current law.	Would prohibit preemption of candidate or party use of broadcast station unless beyond broadcaster's control. Would cap LUC at the maximum amount charged for the same amount of time sold, at any time, during the past 180 days; would limit LUC to the state(s) in which the candidate is seeking election. Would extend LUC to purchases by national party committees if a covered organization spends at least $50,000 for electioneering communications or independent expenditures surrounding a federal election.

Table 1. (Continued).

Major Policy Issue	Overview of Major Relevant Provisions in Current Federal Law	Overview of Major Provisions in H.R. 5175 as Passed by the House	Overview of Major Provisions in S. 3628 as Introduced in the Senate	Overview of Major Provisions in S. 3295 as Introduced in the Senate
Judicial Review	The Bipartisan Campaign Reform Act of 2002 (BCRA) provides that if the constitutionality of the Act is challenged, the action shall be filed in U.S. District Court for D.C., heard by a 3-judge court, reviewable only by direct appeal to the U.S. Supreme Court, requires courts to advance on the docket and expedite the disposition of the action and appeal; provides that any Member of the House or Senate shall have the right to intervene or bring suit challenging the constitutionality. [Bipartisan Campaign Reform Act (BCRA), P.L. 107-155, § 403]	Would provide that if constitutionality of the Act is challenged, the action shall be filed in U.S. District Court for D.C. and appealed to the Court of Appeals for the D.C. Circuit; any Member of House or Senate, who satisfies requirements for standing under Art. III of the U.S. Constitution, shall have right to intervene in any action challenging the Act's constitutionality; any Member of House or Senate may bring suit challenging the constitutionality. [§ 401]	Substantially similar to H.R. 5175.	Would require random audits of LUC functioning and require broadcasters to make LUC requests publicly available via the Internet. [§ 401] Substantially similar to H.R. 5175 and S. 3628, however would also require courts to advance on the docket and expedite the disposition of the action; and would provide that any Member of the House or Senate shall have the right to intervene. [§ 501]

Major Policy Issue	Overview of Major Relevant Provisions in Current Federal Law	Overview of Major Provisions in H.R. 5175 as Passed by the House	Overview of Major Provisions in S. 3628 as Introduced in the Senate	Overview of Major Provisions in S. 3295 as Introduced in the Senate
No Effect on Protections Against Threats, Harassments, and Reprisals	According to Supreme Court precedent, disclosure requirements cannot constitutionally be required where there is a reasonable probability that compelled disclosure would subject contributors to threats, harassment, or reprisals from either government officials or private parties, [Buckley v. Valeo, 424 U.S. 1, 74 (1976); see also, Brown v. Socialist Workers '74 Campaign Comm., 459 U.S. 87, 93-94 (1982)].	Would provide that nothing in the Act shall be construed to affect any law, rule, or regulation that waives a requirement to disclose information relating to any person where there is a reasonable probability that the disclosure would subject person to threats, harassments, or reprisals. [§ 402]	Substantially similar to H.R. 5175.	No comparable provision.
Severability	The Bipartisan Campaign Reform Act of 2002 (BCRA) provides that if any provision of the Act or application of a provision is held unconstitutional, the remainder the Act shall not be affected by the holding. [Bipartisan Campaign Reform Act of 2002 (BCRA), P.L. 107-155, § 401]	Would specify that if any provision of the Act or application of a provision is held unconstitutional, the remainder shall not be affected by the holding. [§ 403]	Substantially similar to H.R. 5175.	Substantially similar to H.R. 5175 and S. 3628. [§ 502]

Source: CRS analysis of H.R. 5175, S. 3295, S. 3628, and current federal campaign finance law, or applicable regulations as noted.

Note: H.R. 5175, S. 3295, and S. 3628 would change the definitions of *independent expenditures* and *electioneering communications*. Thus, the terms do not have the same meanings in all the columns. The column describing major provisions in current law uses the terms *independent expenditures* and *electioneering communications* as defined under existing law, while the column describing major provisions in H.R. 5175, S. 3295 and S. 3628 uses the expanded definitions of the terms as set forth in the legislation.

a. Under IRC § 527, an exempt function is the "influence[ing] or attempt[ing] to influence the selection, nomination, election, or appointment of an individual to a federal, state, or local public office, to an office in a political organization, or as a Presidential or Vice-Presidential elector." Under current law, any § 501(c) organization that makes an expenditure for an exempt function activity is subject to a 35% tax on the lesser of its net investment income or the expenditure. An organization may avoid the tax by setting up a separate segregated fund under IRC § 527(f)(3) to make the expenditures.

End Notes

[1] On the development of federal campaign finance policy and law, see, for example, Kurt Hohenstein, *Coining Corruption: The Making of the American Campaign Finance System* (DeKalb, IL: Northern Illinois University Press, 2007); Robert E. Mutch, *Campaigns, Congress, and Courts: The Making of Federal Campaign Finance Law* (New York: Praeger, 1988); Raymond J. La Raja, *Small Change: Money, Political Parties, and Campaign Finance Reform* (Ann Arbor, MI: University of Michigan Press, 2008); and John Samples, *The Fallacy of Campaign Finance Reform* (Chicago: University of Chicago Press, 2006).

[2] See, for example, Stephen Ansolabehere, Roy Behr, and Shanto Iyengar, *The Media Game: American Politics in the Television Age* (New York: Macmillan, 1993); and *Crowded Airwaves: Campaign Advertising in Elections*, eds. James A. Thurber, Candice J. Nelson, and David A. Dulio (Washington: Brookings Institution Press, 2000).

[3] 130 S. Ct. 876 (2010).

[4] This report does not provide a constitutional analysis and does not address all policy or legal factors that might be relevant for Congress. For analysis of the constitutionality of possible legislative responses to *Citizens United*, see CRS Report R41096, *Legislative Options After Citizens United v. FEC: Constitutional and Legal Issues*, by L. Paige Whitaker et al. For analysis of the policy implications of various legislative options, see CRS Report R41054, *Campaign Finance Policy After Citizens United v. Federal Election Commission: Issues and Options for Congress*, by R. Sam Garrett.

[5] 2 U.S.C. § 431 (17).

[6] 2 U.S.C. § 434(f)(3).

[7] 2 U.S.C. § 441b(a).

[8] 34 Stat. 864.

[9] 61 Stat. 136.

[10] Codified as amended at 2 U.S.C. § 431 *et seq.*

[11] 2 U.S.C. § 441b(b)(2)(C).

[12] 424 U.S. 1 (1976).

[13] For a historical overview, see, for example, Anthony Corrado et al., *The New Campaign Finance Sourcebook* (Washington: Brookings Institution Press, 2005), pp. 35-47.

[14] 551 U.S. 449 (2007). For additional discussion, see CRS Report RS22687, The Constitutionality of Regulating Political Advertisements: An Analysis of Federal Election Commission v. Wisconsin Right to Life, Inc., by L. Paige Whitaker; and CRS Report RL34324, Campaign Finance: Legislative Developments and Policy Issues in the 110th Congress, by R. Sam Garrett.

[15] 130 S. Ct. 876 (2010). For additional discussion, see CRS Report R41045, The Constitutionality of Regulating Corporate Expenditures: A Brief Analysis of the Supreme Court Ruling in Citizens United v. FEC, by L. Paige Whitaker.

[16] *Id.* at 898.

[17] 494 U.S. 652 (1990).

[18] 540 U.S. 93 (2003).

[19] See Citizens United, 130 S. Ct. at 912-14 . For further discussion of McConnell v. FEC and Austin v. Michigan Chamber of Commerce, see CRS Report RL30669, The Constitutionality of Campaign Finance Regulation: Buckley v. Valeo and Its Supreme Court Progeny, by L. Paige Whitaker.

[20] *See id.* at 913-15.

[21] *Id.* at 914 (quoting Buckley v. Valeo, 424 U.S. 1, 64 (1976)).

[22] *See* 2 U.S.C. § 441i(a).

[23] For an overview of the questions and points of debate referenced in this section, see, for example U.S. Congress, House Committee on House Administration, *DISCLOSE Act*, report to accompany H.R. 5175, 111th Cong., 2nd sess., May 25, 2010, H.Rept. 111-492 (Washington: GPO, 2010).

[24] An exception existed for *qualified nonprofit corporations*, which were defined as a § 501(c)(4) corporation meeting the following criteria: (1) its only express purpose is the promotion of political ideas;v44 (2) it cannot engage in business activities; (3) it has no shareholders or other persons with an ownership interest or claim on the organization's assets or who receive any benefit from the corporation that is a disincentive for them to disassociate themselves from the corporation's position on a political issue; and (4) it was not established by and does not accept donations from business corporations. 11 C.F.R. § 114.10(c). The regulatory criteria for "qualified nonprofit corporations" is based on the U.S. Supreme Court ruling in *FEC v. Massachusetts Citizens for Life, Inc. (MCFL)*, 479 U.S. 238 (1986), holding that the FECA prohibition on corporations using

their treasury funds to make independent expenditures could not constitutionally be applied to certain non-profit corporations.

[25] See CRS Report R41054, Campaign Finance Policy After Citizens United v. Federal Election Commission: Issues and Options for Congress, by R. Sam Garrett.

[26] Thus far, the Senate Committee on Rules and Administration and Committee on the Judiciary have both held *Citizens United* hearings, although those hearings did not address specific legislation per se.

[27] The Committee reported the bill on May 25, *see* U.S. Congress, House Committee on House Administration, *DISCLOSE Act*, report to accompany H.R. 5175, 111th Cong., 2nd sess., May 25, 2010, H.Rept. 111-492 (Washington: GPO, 2010). Also in the House, on March 11, the Committee on Financial Services, Subcommittee on Capital Markets, Insurance, and Government Sponsored Enterprises, held a hearing addressing corporate governance and shareholder protection after *Citizens United.* In addition to exploring general themes, various legislative proposals, including Representative Capuano's Shareholder Protection Act (H.R. 4790), were discussed. At the May 20, 2010, Committee on House Administration markup, Rep. Capuano initially offered the Shareholder Protection Act as an amendment to the DISCLOSE Act. He ultimately withdrew the amendment, saying that it would be pursued separately.

[28] U.S. Congress, House Committee on House Administration, *DISCLOSE Act*, report to accompany H.R. 5175, 111th Cong., 2nd sess., May 25, 2010, Rept. 111-492 (Washington: GPO, 2010).

[29] "Democracy is Strengthened by Casting Light on Spending in Elections Act," House vote 391, *Congressional Record*, daily edition, vol. 156 (June 24, 2010), p. H4828.

[30] For additional discussion of automated political calls, see CRS Report RL34361, *Automated Political Telephone Calls ("Robo Calls") in Federal Campaigns: Overview and Policy Options*, by R. Sam Garrett and Kathleen Ann Ruane.

[31] H.R. 5175, as introduced and as reported from the Committee on House Administration, § 2.

[32] The House bill also initially contained a $50,000 threshold, which was increased to $7 million in the version reported by the Committee on House Administration, and then to $10 million in the manager's amendment approved by the House.

[33] 47 U.S.C. § 315(b).

[34] *Political committees* include candidate committees, party committees, and political action committees (PACs).

[35] 2 U.S.C. § 432(g). For additional discussion, see CRS Report R40091, *Campaign Finance: Potential Legislative and Policy Issues for the 111th Congress*, by R. Sam Garrett.

[36] See, for example, Letter from Joan D. Aikens, et al., Former Members of the Federal Election Commission, to Reps. Robert Brady and Dan Lungren, Committee on House Administration, May 19, 2010, http://www.campaignfreedom.org/docLib/20100519_DISCLOSEcomments05192010.pdf.

[37] DISCLOSE Act, § 201.

[38] Section 501(c)(4) organizations include social welfare organizations; § 501(c)(5) describes labor, agricultural and horticultural organizations; and § 501(c)(6) organizations include trade associations.

[39] IRC § 527 provides tax-exempt status to *political organizations*, which are entities or funds that are organized and operated primarily to influence "the selection, nomination, election, or appointment of any individual to any Federal, State, or local public office or office in a political organization, or the election of Presidential or Vice-Presidential electors.... " Under FECA, *political committee* is defined to include "any committee, club, association, or other group of persons which receives contributions aggregating in excess of $1,000 during a calendar year or which makes expenditures aggregating in excess of $1,000 during a calendar year," with both *contribution* and *expenditure* defined as monies or anything of value "for the purpose of influencing any election for Federal office." 2 U.S.C. § 431(4)(A), (8)(A), (9)(A). With respect to entities engaging in federal election activity, § 527 *political organizations* include the entities that are regulated as *political committees* under FECA. However, *political organization* is broader than *political committee*, in part because it also includes the groups colloquially referred to as 527s that have been controversial in recent years because they appear intended to influence federal elections in ways that may place them outside the definition of political committee. For more information on 527s, *see* CRS Report RS22895, *527 Groups and Campaign Activity: Analysis Under Campaign Finance and Tax Laws*, by L. Paige Whitaker and Erika K. Lunder.

[40] IRC § 501(c)(3) describes organizations organized and operated for charitable, educational, and religious purposes, among others.

[41] IRC § 501(c)(3) (prohibiting the organizations described therein from "participat[ing] in, or intervene[ing] in ... any political campaign on behalf of (or in opposition to) any candidate for public office").

[42] For more information, see CRS Report R40141, *501(c)(3) Organizations and Campaign Activity: Analysis Under Tax and Campaign Finance Laws*, by Erika K. Lunder and L. Paige Whitaker.

[43] *See* Rev. Rul. 2004-6.

[44] This figure was obtained by dividing the total contract dollars awarded by the total number of contracts, as reported on USASpending.gov. *See* http://www.usaspending.gov/explore?carryfilters= on&trendreport= top_cont&fromfiscal= yes&tab=By+Recipient&fiscal_year=2009&tab=By+Recipient&fiscal_year=2008&fromfiscal=yes&carryfilters=on& Submit=Go.

[45] For purposes of federal procurement, a "small" business is one that is independently owned and operated, is "not dominant in its field of operation," and meets any definitions or standards established by the Small Business Administration. 15 U.S.C. § 632(a)(1)-(2)(A). These standards focus primarily upon the size of the business, as measured by the number of employees, its annual average gross income, and the size of other businesses within the same industry. 13 C.F.R. §§ 121.101-121.108. For example, businesses in the field of scheduled passenger air transportation are small if they have fewer than 1,500 employees, while those in the data processing field are small if they have a gross income of less than $25 million. 13 C.F.R. § 121.201.

[46] The relevant provisions of the DISCLOSE Act appear to apply to the value of each individual contract, not the total value of contracts received by a particular contractor. However, it is unclear whether the value is measured in terms of the base contract, or all options under the contract.

[47] 15 U.S.C. § 637 note; 48 C.F.R. § 19.805-1(b)(2). Certain group-owned 8(a) firms are not subject to even these limitations and may receive sole-source contracts of any value.

[48] Gov't Accountability Office, Contract Management: Increased Use of Alaska Native Corporations' Special 8(a) Provisions Calls for Tailored Oversight, GAO-06-399, April 2006, at 15, *available at* http://www.gao.gov/new.items/ d06399.pdf (reporting a $593 million sole-source award to Chugach Management Services, Inc.).

[49] For example, Lockheed Martin Corp., the top federal contractor in FY2009, received five contracts valued at over $1 billion in FY2009. *See* USASpending.gov, http://www.usaspending.gov/explore?tab= By%20 Recipient& contractorid= 359799&fromfiscal=yes&carryfilters=on&fiscal_year=2009.

[50] 12 U.S.C. § 5211 *et seq.*

[51] For additional discussion of coordinated party expenditures, see CRS Report RS22644, *Coordinated Party Expenditures in Federal Elections: An Overview*, by R. Sam Garrett and L. Paige Whitaker.

[52] 2 U.S.C. § 434(c)(2)(C); 11 C.F.R. § 109.10.

[53] In general, these groups are required to periodically report to the IRS any expenditure of at least $500 and donors who have given at least $200 during the year. IRC § 527(j). These requirements do not apply to independent expenditures. For more information, see CRS Report RS21716, *Political Organizations Under Section 527 of the Internal Revenue Code*, by Erika K. Lunder; CRS Report RS20918, *527 Organizations and Campaign Activity: Timing of Reporting Requirements under Tax and Campaign Finance Laws*, by Erika K. Lunder and L. Paige Whitaker.

[54] DISCLOSE Act, § 213.

[55] 2 U.S.C. § 439a(a)(3). These provisions apply to permissible use of candidate campaign committee funds, suggesting that amendment would be required to make them applicable to campaign-related-activity accounts.

[56] 2 U.S.C. § 437c(b).

[57] Some primary elections have already occurred without FEC action or legislation implementing the Court's decision in *Citizens United*. Those who believe that the case marked a victory for protected speech might contend that an apparent lack of overwhelming new advertising could be evidence that additional regulation or legislation responding to the ruling is unnecessary or it could be that potential participants are remaining on the sidelines until the state of the law appears more settled.

[58] For a brief overview of Commission duties requiring consensus among at least four Commissioners, see CRS Report RS22780, *The Federal Election Commission (FEC) With Fewer than Four Members: Overview of Policy Implications*, by R. Sam Garrett.

[59] For an overview of deadlocked votes during the current Commission's first year, between July 2008 and June 2009, see CRS Report R40779, *Deadlocked Votes Among Members of the Federal Election Commission (FEC): Overview and Potential Considerations for Congress*, by R. Sam Garrett. Deadlocks have continued on some matters since that time.

In: The DISCLOSE Act and Campaign Finance
Editor: Danielle P. Cacinello

ISBN: 978-1-61324-016-8

Chapter 2

THE DISCLOSE ACT - FROM THE HOUSE OF REPRESENTATIVES, 111TH CONGRESS*

From the House Reports Online via GPO Access

111th Congress Rept. 111-492
HOUSE OF REPRESENTATIVES
2d Session Part 1

DISCLOSE ACT

May 25, 2010.--Committed to the Committee of the Whole House on the State of the Union and ordered to be printed

Mr. Brady of Pennsylvania, from the Committee on House Administration, submitted the following

R E P O R T

together with
MINORITY VIEWS

[To accompany H.R. 5175]

[Including cost estimate of the Congressional Budget Office]

* This is an edited reformatted and augmented version of a House of Representatives publication, report 111-492, dated May 25, 2010.

The Committee on House Administration, to whom was referred the bill (H.R. 5175) to amend the Federal Election Campaign Act of 1971 to prohibit foreign influence in Federal elections, to prohibit government contractors from making expenditures with respect to such elections, and to establish additional disclosure requirements with respect to spending in such elections, and for other purposes, having considered the same, report favorably thereon with an amendment and recommend that the bill as amended do pass.

The amendment is as follows:
Strike all after the enacting clause and insert the following:

SECTION 1. SHORT TITLE; TABLE OF CONTENTS.

(a) Short Title.--This Act may be cited as the ``Democracy is Strengthened by Casting Light on Spending in Elections Act'' or the ``DISCLOSE Act''.
(b) Table of Contents.--The table of contents of this Act is as follows:

Title I--Regulation 0f Certain Political Spending

Title II--Promoting Effective Disclosure of Campaign-Related Activity

Subtitle A--Treatment of Independent Expenditures and Electioneering Communications Made by All Persons

Subtitle B--Expanded Requirements for Corporations and Other Organizations

SEC. 2. FINDINGS

(a) General Findings.--Congress finds and declares as follows:

(1) Throughout the history of the United States, the American people have been rightly concerned about the power of special interests to control our democratic processes. That was true over 100 years ago when Congress first enacted legislation intended to restrict corporate funds from being used in Federal elections, legislation that Congress amended in 1947 to expressly include independent expenditures. The Supreme Court held such legislation to be constitutional in 1990 in Austin v. Michigan Chamber of Commerce (494 U.S. 652) and again in 2003 in McConnell v. F.E.C. (540 U.S. 93).

(2) The Supreme Court's decision in Citizens United v. Federal Election Commission on January 21, 2010, invalidated legislation restricting the ability of corporations and labor unions to spend funds from their general treasury accounts to influence the outcome of elections.

(b) Findings Relating to Government Contractors.--Congress finds and declares as follows:

(1) Government contracting is an activity that is particularly susceptible to improper influence, and to the appearance of improper influence. Government contracts must be awarded based on an objective evaluation of how well bidders or potential contractors meet relevant statutory criteria.

(2) Independent expenditures and electioneering communications that benefit particular candidates or elected officials or disfavor their opponents can lead to apparent and actual ingratiation, access, influence, and quid pro quo arrangements. Government contracts should be awarded based on an objective application of statutory criteria, not based on other forms of inappropriate or corrupting influence.

(3) Prohibiting independent expenditures and electioneering communications by persons negotiating for or performing government contracts will prevent government officials involved in or with influence over the contracting process from influencing the contracting process based, consciously or otherwise, on this kind of inappropriate or corrupting influence.

(4) Prohibiting independent expenditures and electioneering communications by persons negotiating for or performing government contracts will likewise prevent such persons from feeling pressure, whether actually exerted by government officials or not, to make expenditures and to fund communications in order to maximize their chances of receiving contracts, or to match similar expenditures and communications made by their competitors.

(5) Furthermore, because government contracts often involve large amounts of public money, it is critical that the public perceive that the government contracts are awarded strictly in accordance with prescribed statutory standards, and not based on other forms of inappropriate or corrupting influence. The public's confidence in government is undermined when corporations that make significant expenditures during Federal election campaigns later receive government funds.

(6) Prohibiting independent expenditures and electioneering communications by persons negotiating for or performing government contracts will prevent any appearance that government contracts were awarded based in whole or in part on such expenditures or communications, or based on the inappropriate or corrupting influence such expenditures and communications can create and appear to create.

(7) In these ways, prohibiting independent expenditures and electioneering communications by persons negotiating for or performing government contracts will protect the actual and perceived integrity of the government contracting process.

(8) Moreover, the risks of waste, fraud and abuse, all resulting in economic losses to taxpayers, are significant when would-be public contractors or applicants for public funds make expenditures in Federal election campaigns in order to affect electoral outcomes.

(c) Findings Relating to Foreign Corporations.--Congress finds and declares as follows:

(1) The Supreme Court's decision in the Citizens United case has provided the means by which United States corporations controlled by foreign entities can freely spend money to influence United States elections.

(2) Foreign corporations commonly own U.S. corporations in whole or in part, and U.S. corporate equity and debt are also held by foreign individuals, sovereign wealth funds, and even foreign nations at levels which permit effective control over those U.S. entities.

(3) As recognized in many areas of the law, foreign ownership interests and influences are exerted in a perceptible way even when the entity is not majority-foreign-owned.

(4) The Federal Government has broad constitutional power to protect American interests and sovereignty from foreign interference and intrusion.

(5) Congress has a clear interest in minimizing foreign intervention, and the perception of foreign intervention, in United States elections.

(d) Findings Relating to Coordinated Expenditures.--Congress finds and declares as follows:

(1) It has been the consistent view of Congress and the courts that coordinated expenditures in campaigns for election are no different in nature from contributions.

(2) Existing rules still allow donors to evade contribution limits by making campaign expenditures which, while technically qualifying as independent expenditures under law, are for all relevant purposes coordinated with candidates and political parties and thus raise the potential for corruption or the appearance of corruption.

(3) Such arrangements have the potential to give rise to the reality or appearance of corruption to the same degree that direct contributions to a candidate may give rise to the reality or appearance of corruption. Moreover, expenditures which are in fact made in coordination with a candidate or political party have the potential to lessen the public's trust and faith in the rules and the integrity of the electoral process.

(4) The government therefore has a compelling interest in making sure that expenditures that are de facto coordinated with a candidate are treated as such to prevent corruption, the appearance of corruption, or the perception that some participants are circumventing the laws and regulations which govern the financing of election campaigns.

(e) Findings Relating to Disclosures and Disclaimers.--Congress finds and declares as follows:

(1) The American people have a compelling interest in knowing who is funding independent expenditures and electioneering communications to influence Federal elections, and the government has a compelling interest in providing the public with that information. Effective disclaimers and prompt disclosure of expenditures, and the disclosure of the funding sources for these expenditures, can provide shareholders, voters, and citizens with the information needed to evaluate the actions by special interests seeking influence over the democratic process. Transparency promotes accountability, increases the fund of information available to the public concerning the support given to candidates by special interests, sheds the light of publicity on political spending, and encourages the leaders of organizations to act only upon legitimate organizational purposes.

(2) Protecting this compelling interest has become particularly important to address the anticipated increase in special interest spending on election-related communications which will result from the Supreme Court's decision in the Citizens United case. The current disclosure and disclaimer requirements were designed for a campaign finance system in which such expenditures were subject to prohibitions that no longer apply.

(3) More rigorous disclosure and disclaimer requirements are necessary to protect against the evasion of current rules. Organizations that engage in election-related communications have used a variety of methods to attempt to obscure their sponsorship of communications from the general public. Robust disclosure and disclaimer requirements are necessary to ensure that the electorate is informed about who is paying for particular election-related communications, and so that the shareholders and members of these organizations are aware of their organizations' election-related spending.

(4) The current lack of accountability and transparency allow special interest political spending to serve as a private benefit for the officials of special interest organizations, to the detriment of the organizations and their shareholders and members.

(5) Various factors, including the advent of the Internet, where particular communications can be circulated and remain available for viewing long after they are first broadcast, and the frequency of political campaigns that effectively begin long before election day, have also rendered the existing system of disclosure and disclaimer requirements (including the limited time periods during which some of those requirements currently apply) inadequate to protect fully the government's interest in ensuring that the electorate is fully informed about the sources of election-related spending, and that shareholders and citizens alike have the information they need to hold corporations and elected officials accountable for their positions and supporters.

(6) To serve the interests of accountability and transparency, it is also important that information about who is funding independent expenditures and electioneering communications be presented to the electorate in a manner that is readily accessible and that can be quickly and easily understood.

(f) Findings Relating to Campaign Spending by Lobbyists.--Congress finds and declares as follows:

(1) Lobbyists and lobbying organizations, and through them, their clients, influence the public decision-making process in a variety of ways.

(2) In recent years, scandals involving undue lobbyist influence have lowered public trust in government and jeopardized the willingness of voters to take part in democratic governance.

(3) One way in which lobbyists may unduly influence Federal officials is through their or their clients making independent expenditures or electioneering communications targeting elected officials.

(4) Disclosure of such independent expenditures and electioneering communications will allow the public to examine connections between such spending and official actions, and will therefore limit the ability of lobbyists to exert an undue influence on elected officials.

TITLE I--REGULATION OF CERTAIN POLITICAL SPENDING

Sec. 101. Prohibiting Independent Expenditures and Electioneering Communications by Government Contractors.

(a) Prohibition Applicable to Government Contractors.--

(1) Prohibition.--

(A) In general.--Section 317(a)(1) of the Federal Election Campaign Act (2 U.S.C. 441c(a)(1)) is amended by striking ``purpose or use; or'' and inserting the following: ``purpose or use, to make any independent expenditure, or to disburse any funds for an electioneering communication; or''.

(B) Conforming amendment.--The heading of section 317 of such Act (2 U.S.C. 441c) is amended by striking ``contributions'' and inserting ``contributions, independent expenditures, and electioneering communications''.

(2) Threshold for application of ban.--Section 317 of such Act (2 U.S.C. 441c) is amended--

(A) by redesignating subsections (b) and (c) as subsections (c) and (d); and

(B) by inserting after subsection (a) the following new subsection:

``(b) To the extent that subsection (a)(1) prohibits a person who enters into a contract described in such subsection from making any independent expenditure or disbursing funds for an electioneering communication, such subsection shall apply only if the value of the contract is equal to or greater than $7,000,000.''.

(b) Application to Recipients of Assistance Under Troubled Asset Program.--Section 317(a) of such Act (2 U.S.C. 441c(a)) is amended--

(1) by striking ``or'' at the end of paragraph (1);

(2) by redesignating paragraph (2) as paragraph (3); and

(3) by inserting after paragraph (1) the following new paragraph:

``(2) who enters into negotiations for financial assistance under title I of the Emergency Economic Stabilization Act of 2008 (12 U.S.C. 5211 et seq.) (relating to the purchase of troubled assets by the Secretary of the Treasury), during the period--

``(A) beginning on the later of the commencement of the negotiations or the date of the enactment of the Democracy is Strengthened by Casting Light on Spending in Elections Act; and

``(B) ending with the later of the termination of such negotiations or the repayment of such financial assistance; directly or indirectly to make any contribution of money or other things of value, or to promise expressly or impliedly to make any such contribution to any political party, committee, or candidate for public office or to any person for any political purpose or use, to make any independent expenditure, or to disburse any funds for an electioneering communication; or''.

(c) Technical Amendment.--Section 317 of such Act (2 U.S.C. 441c) is amended by striking ``section 321'' each place it appears and inserting ``section 316''.

Sec. 102. Application of Ban on Contributions and Expenditures by Foreign Nationals to Foreign-Controlled Domestic Corporations

(a) Application of Ban.--Section 319(b) of the Federal Election Campaign Act of 1971 (2 U.S.C. 441e(b)) is amended--

(1) by striking ``or'' at the end of paragraph (1);

(2) by striking the period at the end of paragraph (2) and inserting ``; or''; and

(3) by adding at the end the following new paragraph:

``(3) any corporation which is not a foreign national described in paragraph (1) and--

``(A) in which a foreign national described in paragraph (1) or (2) directly or indirectly owns 20 percent or more of the voting shares;

``(B) with respect to which the majority of the members of the board of directors are foreign nationals described in paragraph (1) or (2);

``(C) over which one or more foreign nationals described in paragraph (1) or (2) has the power to direct, dictate, or control the decision-making process of the corporation with respect to its interests in the United States; or

``(D) over which one or more foreign nationals described in paragraph (1) or (2) has the power to direct, dictate, or control the decision-making process of the corporation with respect to activities in connection with a Federal, State, or local election, including--

``(i) the making of a contribution, donation, expenditure, independent expenditure, or disbursement for an electioneering communication (within the meaning of section 304(f)(3)); or

``(ii) the administration of a political committee established or maintained by the corporation.''.

(b) Certification of Compliance.--Section 319 of such Act (2 U.S.C. 441e) is amended by adding at the end the following new subsection:

``(c) Certification of Compliance Required Prior to Carrying Out Activity.--Prior to the making in connection with an election for Federal office of any contribution, donation, expenditure, independent expenditure, or disbursement for an electioneering communication by a corporation during a year, the chief executive officer of the corporation (or, if the corporation does not have a chief executive officer, the highest ranking official of the corporation), shall file a certification with the Commission, under penalty of perjury, that the corporation is not prohibited from carrying out such activity under subsection (b)(3), unless the chief executive officer has previously filed such a certification during the year. Nothing in this subsection shall be construed to apply to any contribution, donation, expenditure, independent expenditure, or disbursement from a separate segregated fund established and administered by a corporation under section 316(b)(2)(C).''.

(c) No Effect on Separate Segregated Funds of Domestic

Corporations.--Section 319 of such Act (2 U.S.C. 441e), as amended by subsection (b), is further amended by adding at the end the following new subsection:

``(d) No Effect on Separate Segregate Funds of Domestic Corporations.--Nothing in this section shall be construed to prohibit any corporation which is not a foreign national described in paragraph (1) of subsection (b) from establishing, administering, and soliciting contributions to a separate segregated fund under section 316(b)(2)(C),

so long as none of the amounts in the fund are provided by any foreign national described in paragraph (1) or (2) of subsection (b) and no foreign national described in paragraph (1) or (2) of subsection (b) has the power to direct, dictate, or control the establishment or administration of the fund.''.

(d) No Effect on Other Laws.--Section 319 of such Act (2 U.S.C. 441e), as amended by subsections (b) and (c), is further amended by adding at the end the following new subsection:

``(e) No Effect on Other Laws.--Nothing in this section shall be construed to affect the determination of whether a corporation is treated as a foreign national for purposes of any law other than this Act.''.

Sec. 103. Treatment of Payments for Coordinated Communications as Contributions

(a) In General.--Section 301(8)(A) of the Federal Election Campaign

Act of 1971 (2 U.S.C. 431(8)(A)) is amended--

(1) by striking ``or'' at the end of clause (i);

(2) by striking the period at the end of clause (ii) and inserting ``; or''; and

(3) by adding at the end the following new clause:

``(iii) any payment made by any person (other than a candidate, an authorized committee of a candidate, or a political committee of a political party) for a coordinated communication (as determined under section 324).''.

(b) Coordinated Communications Described.--Section 324 of such Act (2 U.S.C. 441k) is amended to read as follows:

``Sec. 324. Coordinated Communications

``(a) Coordinated Communications Defined.--For purposes of this Act, the term `coordinated communication' means--

``(1) a covered communication which, subject to subsection (c), is made in cooperation, consultation, or concert with, or at the request or suggestion of, a candidate, an authorized committee of a candidate, or a political committee of a political party; or

``(2) any communication that republishes, disseminates, or distributes, in whole or in part, any broadcast or any written, graphic, or other form of campaign material prepared by a candidate, an authorized committee of a candidate, or their agents.

``(b) Covered Communication Defined.--

``(1) In general.--Except as provided in paragraph (4), for purposes of this subsection, the term `covered communication' means, for purposes of the applicable election period described in paragraph (2), a public communication (as defined in section 301(22)) that refers to a clearly identified candidate for Federal office and is publicly distributed or publicly disseminated during such period.

``(2) Applicable election period.--For purposes of paragraph (1), the `applicable election period' with respect to a communication means--

``(A) in the case of a communication which refers to a candidate for the office of President or Vice President, the period--

``(i) beginning with the date that is 120 days before the date of the first primary election, preference election, or nominating convention for nomination for the office of President which is held in any State; and

``(ii) ending with the date of the general election for such office; or

``(B) in the case of a communication which refers to a candidate for any other Federal office, the period--

``(i) beginning with the date that is 90 days before the earliest of the primary election, preference election, or nominating convention with respect to the nomination for the office that the candidate is seeking; and

``(ii) ending with the date of the general election for such office.

``(3) Special rule for public distribution of communications involving congressional candidates.--For purposes of paragraph (1), in the case of a communication involving a candidate for an office other than President or Vice President, the communication shall be considered to be publicly distributed or publicly disseminated only if the dissemination or distribution occurs in the jurisdiction of the office that the candidate is seeking.

``(4) Exception.--The term `covered communication' does not include--

``(A) a communication appearing in a news story, commentary, or editorial distributed through the facilities of any broadcasting station, newspaper, magazine, or other periodical publication, unless such facilities are owned or controlled by any political party, political committee, or candidate; or

``(B) a communication which constitutes a candidate debate or forum conducted pursuant to the regulations adopted by the Commission to carry out section 304(f)(3)(B)(iii), or which solely promotes such a debate or forum and is made by or on behalf of the person sponsoring the debate or forum.

``(c) No Finding of Coordination Based Solely on Sharing of Information Regarding Legislative or Policy Position.--For purposes of subsection (a)(1), a covered communication may not be considered to be made in cooperation, consultation, or concert with, or at the request or suggestion of, a candidate, an authorized committee of a candidate, or a political committee of a political party solely on the grounds that a person provided information to the candidate or committee regarding that person's position on a legislative or policy matter (including urging the candidate or party to adopt that person's position), so long as there is no discussion between the person and the candidate or committee regarding the candidate's campaign for election for Federal office.

``(d) Preservation of Certain Safe Harbors and Firewalls.--Nothing in this section may be construed to affect 11 CFR 109.21(g) or (h), as in effect on the date of the enactment of the Democracy is Strengthened by Casting Light on Spending in Elections Act.

``(e) Treatment of Coordination With Political Parties for Communications Referring to Candidates.--For purposes of this section, if a communication which refers to any clearly identified candidate or candidates of a political party or any opponent of such a candidate or candidates is determined to have been made in cooperation, consultation, or concert with or at the request or suggestion of a political committee of the political party but not in cooperation, consultation, or concert with or at the request or suggestion of such clearly identified candidate or candidates, the communication shall be treated as having been made in cooperation, consultation, or concert with or at the request or suggestion of the political committee of the political party but not with or at the request or suggestion of such clearly identified candidate or candidates.''.

(c) Effective Date.--

(1) In general.--This section and the amendments made by this section shall apply with respect to payments made on or after the expiration of the 30-day period which begins on the date of the enactment of this Act, without regard to whether or not the Federal Election Commission has promulgated regulations to carry out such amendments.

(2) Transition rule for actions taken prior to enactment.--No person shall be considered to have made a payment for a coordinated communication under section 324 of the Federal Election Campaign Act of 1971 (as amended by subsection (b)) by reason of any action taken by the person prior to the date of the enactment of this Act. Nothing in the previous sentence shall be construed to affect any determination under any other provision of such Act which is in effect on the date of the enactment of this Act regarding whether a communication is made in cooperation, consultation, or concert with, or at the request or suggestion of, a candidate, an authorized committee of a candidate, or a political committee of a political party.

Sec. 104. Treatment of Political Party Communications Made on Behalf of Candidates

(a) Treatment of Payment for Public Communication as Contribution if Made Under Control or Direction of Candidate.--Section 301(8)(A) of the Federal Election Campaign Act of 1971 (2 U.S.C. 431(8)(A)), as amended by section 103(a), is amended--

(1) by striking ``or'' at the end of clause (ii);

(2) by striking the period at the end of clause (iii) and inserting ``; or''; and

(3) by adding at the end the following new clause:

``(iv) any payment by a political committee of a political party for the direct costs of a public communication (as defined in paragraph (22)) made on behalf of a candidate for Federal office who is affiliated with such party, but only if the communication is controlled by, or made at the direction of, the candidate or an authorized committee of the candidate.''.

(b) Requiring Control or Direction by Candidate for Treatment as Coordinated Party Expenditure.--

(1) In general.--Paragraph (4) of section 315(d) of such Act

(2 U.S.C. 441a(d)) is amended to read as follows:

``(4) Special Rule for Direct Costs of Communications.--The direct costs incurred by a political committee of a political party for a communication made in connection with the campaign of a candidate for Federal office shall not be subject to the limitations contained in paragraphs (2) and (3) unless the communication is controlled by, or made at the direction of, the candidate or an authorized committee of the candidate.''.

(2) Conforming amendment.--Paragraph (1) of section 315(d) of such Act (2 U.S.C. 441a(d)) is amended by striking ``paragraphs (2), (3), and (4)'' and inserting ``paragraphs (2) and (3)''.

(c) Effective Date.--This section and the amendments made by this section shall apply with respect to payments made on or after the expiration of the 30-day period which begins on the date of the enactment of this Act, without regard to whether or not the Federal Election Commission has promulgated regulations to carry out such amendments.

Sec. 105. Restriction on Internet Communications Treated as Public Communications

(a) In General.--Section 301(22) of the Federal Election Campaign Act of 1971 (2 U.S.C. 431(22)) is amended by adding at the end the following new sentence: ``A communication which is disseminated through the Internet shall not be treated as a form of general public political advertising under this paragraph unless the communication was placed for a fee on another person's Web site.''.

(b) Effective Date.--The amendment made by subsection (a) shall take effect on the date of the enactment of this Act.

TITLE II--PROMOTING EFFECTIVE DISCLOSURE OF CAMPAIGN-RELATED ACTIVITY

Subtitle A--Treatment of Independent Expenditures and Electioneering Communications Made by All Persons

Sec. 201. Independent Expenditures

(a) Revision of Definition.--Subparagraph (A) of section 301(17) of the Federal Election Campaign Act of 1971 (2 U.S.C. 431(17)) is amended to read as follows:

``(A) that, when taken as a whole, expressly advocates the election or defeat of a clearly identified candidate, or is the functional equivalent of express advocacy because it can be interpreted by a reasonable person only as advocating the election or defeat of a candidate, taking into account whether the communication involved mentions a candidacy, a political party, or a challenger to a candidate, or takes a position on a candidate's character, qualifications, or fitness for office; and''.

(b) Uniform 24-Hour Reporting For Persons Making Independent Expenditures Exceeding $10,000 at Any Time.--Section 304(g) of such Act (2 U.S.C. 434(g)) is amended by striking paragraphs (1) and (2) and inserting the following:

``(1) Independent expenditures exceeding threshold amount.--

``(A) Initial report.--A person (including a political committee) that makes or contracts to make independent expenditures in an aggregate amount equal to or greater than the threshold amount described in paragraph (2) shall electronically file a report describing the expenditures within 24 hours.

``(B) Additional reports.--After a person files a report under subparagraph (A), the person shall electronically file an additional report within 24 hours after each time the person makes or contracts to make independent expenditures in an aggregate amount equal to or greater than the threshold amount with respect to the same election as that to which the initial report relates.

``(2) Threshold amount described.--In paragraph (1), the `threshold amount' means--

``(A) during the period up to and including the 20th day before the date of an election, $10,000; or

``(B) during the period after the 20th day, but more than 24 hours, before the date of an election, $1,000.

``(3) Public availability.--Notwithstanding any other provision of this section, the Commission shall ensure that the information required to be disclosed under this subsection is publicly available through the Commission website not later than 24 hours after receipt in a manner that is downloadable in bulk and machine readable.''.

(c) Effective Date.--

(1) In general.--The amendment made by subsection (a) shall apply with respect to contributions and expenditures made on or after the expiration of the 30-day period which begins on the date of the enactment of this Act, without regard to whether or not the Federal Election Commission has promulgated regulations to carry out such amendments.

(2) Reporting requirements.--The amendment made by subsection

(b) shall apply with respect to reports required to be filed after the date of the enactment of this Act.

Sec. 202. Electioneering Communications

(a) Expansion of Period Covering General Election.--Section 304(f)(3)(A)(i)(II)(aa) of the Federal Election Campaign Act of 1971 (2 U.S.C. 434(f)(3)(A)(i)(II)(aa)) is amended by striking ``60 days'' and inserting ``120 days''.

(b) Mandatory Electronic Filing.--Section 304(f)(1) of such Act (2 U.S.C. 434(f)(1)) is amended-- (1) by striking ``file with'' and inserting ``electronically file with''; and

(2) by adding at the end the following new sentence:

``Notwithstanding any other provision of this section, the Commission shall ensure that the information required to be disclosed under this subsection is publicly available through the Commission website not later than 24 hours after receipt in a manner that is downloadable in bulk and machine readable.''.

(c) Effective Date; Transition for Communications Made Prior to Enactment.--The amendment made by subsection (a) shall apply with respect to communications made on or after the date of the enactment of this Act, without regard to whether or not the Federal Election Commission has promulgated regulations to carry out such amendments, except that no communication which is made prior to the date of the enactment of this Act shall be treated as an electioneering communication under section 304(f)(3)(A)(i)(II) of the Federal Election Campaign Act of 1971 (as amended by subsection (a)) unless the communication would be treated as an electioneering communication under such section if the amendment made by subsection (a) did not apply.

Sec. 203. Mandatory Electronic Filing by Persons Making Independent Expenditures or Electioneering Communications Exceeding $10,000 at Any Time

Section 304(d)(1) of the Federal Election Campaign Act of 1971 (2 U.S.C. 434(d)(1)) is amended--

(1) by striking ``or (g)''; and

(2) by adding at the end the following: ``Notwithstanding any other provision of this section, any person who is required to file a statement under subsection (f) or subsection (g) shall file the statement in electronic form accessible by computers, in a manner which ensures that the information provided is searchable, sortable, and downloadable.''.

Subtitle B--Expanded Requirements for Corporations and Other Organizations

Sec. 211. Additional Information Required to Be Included in Reports on Disbursements by Covered Organizations

(a) Independent Expenditure Reports.--Section 304(g) of the Federal Election Campaign Act of 1971 (2 U.S.C. 434(g)) is amended by adding at the end the following new paragraph:

``(5) Disclosure of additional information by covered organizations making payments for public independent expenditures.--

``(A) Additional information.--If a covered organization makes or contracts to make public independent expenditures in an aggregate amount equal to or exceeding $10,000 in a calendar year, the report filed by the organization under this subsection shall include, in addition to the information required under paragraph (3), the following information:

``(i) If any person made a donation or payment to the covered organization during the covered organization reporting period which was provided for the purpose of being used for campaign-related activity or in response to a solicitation for funds to be used for campaign-related activity--

``(I) subject to subparagraph (C), the identification of each person who made such donations or payments in an aggregate amount equal to or exceeding $600 during such period, presented in the order of the aggregate amount of donations or payments made by such persons during such period (with the identification of the person making the largest donation or payment appearing first); and

``(II) if any person identified under subclause (I) designated that the donation or payment be used for campaign-related activity with respect to a specific election or in support of a specific candidate, the name of the election or candidate involved, and if any such person designated that the donation or payment be used for a specific public independent expenditure, a description of the expenditure.

``(ii) The identification of each person who made unrestricted donor payments to the organization during the covered organization reporting period--

``(I) in an aggregate amount equal to or exceeding $600 during such period, if any of the disbursements made by the organization for any of the public independent expenditures which are covered by the report were not made from the organization's Campaign- Related Activity Account under section 326; or

``(II) in an aggregate amount equal to or exceeding $6,000 during such period, if the disbursements made by the organization for all of the public independent expenditures which are covered by the report were made exclusively from the organization's Campaign-Related Activity Account under section 326 (but only if the organization has made deposits described in subparagraph (D) of section 326(a)(2) into that Account during such period in an aggregate amount equal to or greater than $10,000), presented in the order of the aggregate amount of payments made by such persons during such period (making the largest payment appearing first).

``(B) Treatment of transfers made to other persons.--

``(i) In general.--For purposes of the requirement to file reports under this subsection (including the requirement under subparagraph (A) to include additional information in such reports), a covered organization which transfers amounts to another person (other than the covered organization itself) for the purpose of making a public independent expenditure by that person or by any other person, or (in accordance with clause (ii)) which is deemed to have transferred amounts to another person (other than the covered organization itself) for the purpose of making a public independent expenditure by that person or by any other person, shall be considered to have made a public independent expenditure.

``(ii) Rules for deeming transfers made for purpose of making expenditures.--For purposes of clause (i), in determining whether a covered organization or any other person who transfers amounts to another person shall be deemed to have transferred the amounts for the purpose of making a public independent expenditure, the following rules apply:

``(I) The person shall be deemed to have transferred the amounts for the purpose of making a public independent expenditure if-- ``

(aa) the person designates, requests, or suggests that the amounts be used for public independent expenditures and the person to whom the amounts were transferred agrees to do so or does so;

``(bb) the person making the public independent expenditure or another person acting on that person's behalf expressly solicited the person for a donation or payment for making or paying for any public independent expenditures;

``(cc) the person and the person to whom the amounts were transferred engaged in substantial written or oral discussion regarding the person either making, or donating or paying for, any public independent expenditures;

``(dd) the person or the person to whom the amounts were transferred knew or had reason to know of the covered organization's intent to make public independent expenditures; or

``(ee) the person or the person to whom the amounts were transferred made a public independent expenditure during the 2-year period which ends on the date on which the amounts were transferred.

``(II) The person shall not be deemed to have transferred the amounts for the purpose of making a public independent expenditure if the transfer was a commercial transaction occurring in the ordinary course of business between the person and the person to whom the amounts were transferred, unless there is affirmative evidence that the amounts were transferred for the purpose of making a public independent expenditure.

``(C) Exclusion of amounts designated for other campaign-related activity.--For purposes of subparagraph (A)(i), in determining the amount of a donation or payment made by a person which was provided for the purpose of being used for campaign-related activity or in response to a solicitation for funds to be used for campaign-related activity, there shall be excluded any amount which was designated by the person

to be used--

``(i) for campaign-related activity described in clause (i) of section 325(d)(2)(A) (relating to independent expenditures) with respect to a different election, or with respect to a candidate in a different election, than an election which is the subject of any of the public independent expenditures covered by the report involved; or

``(ii) for any campaign-related activity described in clause (ii) of section 325(d)(2)(A) (relating to electioneering communications).

``(D) Exclusion of amounts paid from separate segregated fund.--In determining the amount of public independent expenditures made by a covered organization for purposes of this paragraph, there shall be excluded any amounts paid from a separate segregated fund established and administered by the organization under section 316(b)(2)(C).

``(E) Covered organization reporting period described.--In this paragraph, the `covered organization reporting period' is, with respect to a report filed by a covered organization under this subsection--

``(i) in the case of the first report filed by a covered organization under this subsection which includes information required under this paragraph, the shorter of--

``(I) the period which begins on the effective date of the Democracy is Strengthened by Casting Light on Spending in Elections Act and ends on the last day covered by the report, or

``(II) the 12-month period ending on the last day covered by the report; and ``(ii) in the case of any subsequent report filed by a covered organization under this subsection which includes information required under this paragraph, the period occurring since the most recent report filed by the organization which includes such information.

``(F) Covered organization defined.--In this paragraph, the term `covered organization' means any of the following:

``(i) Any corporation which is subject to section 316(a).

``(ii) Any labor organization (as defined in section 316).

``(iii) Any organization described in paragraph (4), (5), or (6) of section 501(c) of the Internal Revenue Code of 1986 and exempt from tax under section 501(a) of such Code.

``(iv) Any political organization under section 527 of the Internal Revenue Code of 1986, other than a political committee under this Act.

``(G) Other definitions.--In this paragraph--

``(i) the terms `campaign-related activity' and `unrestricted donor payment' have the meaning given such terms in section 325; and

``(ii) the term `public independent expenditure' means an independent expenditure for a public communication (as defined in section 301(22)).''.

(b) Electioneering Communication Reports.--

(1) In general.--Section 304(f) of such Act (2 U.S.C. 434(f)) is amended--

(A) by redesignating paragraphs (6) and (7) as paragraphs (7) and (8); and

(B) by inserting after paragraph (5) the end the following new paragraph:

``(6) Disclosure of additional information by covered organizations.--

``(A) Additional information.--If a covered organization files a statement under this subsection, the statement shall include, in addition to the information required under paragraph (2), the following information:

``(i) If any person made a donation or payment to the covered organization during the covered organization reporting period which was provided for the purpose of being used for campaign-related activity or in response to a solicitation for funds to be used for campaign-related activity--

``(I) subject to subparagraph (C), the identification of each person who made such donations or payments in an aggregate amount equal to or exceeding $1,000 during such period, presented in the order of the aggregate amount of donations or payments made by such persons during such period (with the identification of the person making the largest donation or payment appearing first); and

``(II) if any person identified under subclause (I) designated that the donation or payment be used for campaign-related activity with respect to a specific election or in support of a specific candidate, the name of the election or candidate involved, and if any such person designated that the donation or payment be used for a specific electioneering communication, a description of the communication.

``(ii) The identification of each person who made unrestricted donor payments to the organization during the covered organization reporting period--

``(I) in an aggregate amount equal to or exceeding $1,000 during such period, if any of the disbursements made by the organization for any of the electioneering communications which are covered by the statement were not made from the organization's Campaign-Related Activity Account under section 326; or

``(II) in an aggregate amount equal to or exceeding $10,000 during such period, if the disbursements made by the organization for all of the electioneering communications which are covered by the statement were made exclusively from the organization's Campaign-Related Activity Account under section 326 (but only if the organization has made deposits described in subparagraph (D) of section 326(a)(2) into that Account during such period in an aggregate amount equal to or greater than $10,000),

presented in the order of the aggregate amount of payments made by such persons during such period (with the identification of the person making the largest payment appearing first).

``(B) Treatment of transfers made to other persons.--

``(i) In general.--For purposes of the requirement to file statements under this subsection (including the requirement under subparagraph (A) to include additional information in such statements), a covered organization which transfers amounts to another person (other than the covered organization itself) for the purpose of making an electioneering communication by that person or by any other person, or (in accordance with clause (ii)) which is deemed to have transferred amounts to another person (other than the covered organization itself) for the purpose of making an electioneering communication by that person or by any other person, shall be considered to have made a disbursement for an electioneering communication. ``(ii) Rules for deeming transfers made for purpose of making communications.--For purposes of clause (i), in determining whether a covered organization or any other person who transfers amounts to another person shall be deemed to have transferred the amounts for the purpose of making an electioneering communication, the following rules apply:

``(I) The person shall be deemed to have transferred the amounts for the purpose of making an electioneering communication if--

``(aa) the person designates, requests, or suggests that the amounts be used for electioneering communications and the person to whom the amounts were transferred agrees to do so or does so;

``(bb) the person making the electioneering communication or another person acting on that person's behalf expressly solicited the person for a donation or payment for making or paying for any electioneering communications;

``(cc) the person and the person to whom the amounts were transferred engaged in substantial written or oral discussion regarding the person either making, or donating or paying for, any electioneering communications;

``(dd) the person or the person to whom the amounts were transferred knew or had reason to know of the covered organization's intent to make electioneering communications;

or

``(ee) the person or the person to whom the amounts were transferred made an electioneering communication during the 2-year period which ends on the date on which the amounts were transferred.

``(II) The person shall not be considered to have transferred the amounts for the purpose of making an electioneering communication if the transfer was a commercial transaction occurring in the ordinary course of business between the person and the person to whom the amounts were transferred, unless there is affirmative evidence that the amounts were transferred for the purpose of making an electioneering communication.

``(C) Exclusion of amounts designated for other campaign-related activity.--For purposes of subparagraph (A)(i), in determining the amount of a donation or payment made by a person which was provided for the purpose of being used for campaign-related activity or in response to a solicitation for funds to be used for campaign-related activity, there shall be excluded any amount which was designated by the person to be used--

``(i) for campaign-related activity described in clause (ii) of section 325(d)(2)(A) (relating to electioneering communications) with respect to a different election, or with respect to a candidate in a different election, than an election which is the subject of any of the electioneering communications covered by the statement involved; or

``(ii) for any campaign-related activity described in clause (i) of section 325(d)(2)(A) (relating to independent expenditures consisting of a public communication).

``(D) Covered organization reporting period described.--In this paragraph, the `covered organization reporting period' is, with respect to a statement filed by a covered organization under this subsection--

``(i) in the case of the first statement filed by a covered organization under this subsection which includes information required under this paragraph, the shorter of--

``(I) the period which begins on the effective date of the Democracy is Strengthened by Casting Light on Spending in Elections Act and ends on the disclosure date for the statement, or

``(II) the 12-month period ending on the disclosure date for the statement; and

``(ii) in the case of any subsequent statement filed by a covered organization under this subsection which includes information required under this paragraph, the period occurring since the most recent statement filed by the organization which includes such information.

``(E) Covered organization defined.--In this paragraph, the term `covered organization' means any of the following:

``(i) Any corporation which is subject to section 316(a).

``(ii) Any labor organization (as defined in section 316).

``(iii) Any organization described in paragraph (4), (5), or (6) of section 501(c) of the Internal Revenue Code of 1986 and exempt from tax under section 501(a) of such Code.

``(iv) Any political organization under section 527 of the Internal Revenue Code of 1986, other than a political committee under this Act.

``(F) Other definitions.--In this paragraph, the terms `campaign-related activity' and `unrestricted donor payment' have the meaning given such terms in section 325.''.

(2) Conforming amendment.--Section 304(2) of such Act (2 U.S.C. 434(f)(2)) is amended by striking ``If the disbursements'' each place it appears in subparagraph (E) and (F) and inserting the following: ``Except in the case of a statement which is required to include additional information under paragraph (6), if the disbursements''.

Sec. 212. Rules Regarding Use of General Treasury Funds by Covered Organizations for Campaign-Related Activity

Title III of the Federal Election Campaign Act of 1971 (2 U.S.C. 431 et seq.) is amended by adding at the end the following new section:

``Sec. 325. Special Rules for Use of General Treasury Funds by Covered Organizations for Campaign-Related Activity

``(a) Use of Funds for Campaign-Related Activity.--

``(1) In general.--Subject to any applicable restrictions and prohibitions under this Act, a covered organization may make disbursements for campaign-related activity using--

``(A) amounts paid or donated to the organization which are designated by the person providing the amounts to be used for campaign-related activity;

``(B) unrestricted donor payments made to the organization; and

``(C) other funds of the organization, including amounts received pursuant to commercial activities in the regular course of a covered organization's business.

``(2) No effect on use of separate segregated fund.--Nothing in this section shall be construed to affect the authority of a covered organization to make disbursements from a separate segregated fund established and administered by the organization under section 316(b)(2)(C).

``(b) Mutually Agreed Restrictions on Use of Funds for Campaign-Related Activity.--

``(1) Agreement and certification.--If a covered organization and a person mutually agree, at the time the person makes a donation, payment, or transfer to the organization which would require the organization to disclose the person's identification under section 304(g)(5)(A)(ii) or section 304(f)(6)(A)(ii), that the organization will not use the donation, payment, or transfer for campaign-related activity, then not later than 30 days after the organization receives the donation, payment, or transfer the organization shall transmit to the person a written certification by the chief financial officer of the covered organization (or, if the organization does not have a chief financial officer, the highest ranking financial official of the organization) that--

``(A) the organization will not use the donation, payment, or transfer for campaign-related activity; and

``(B) the organization will not include any information on the person in any report filed by the organization under section 304 with respect to independent expenditures or electioneering communications, so that the person will not be required to appear in a significant funder statement or a Top 5 Funders list under section 318(e).

``(2) Exception for payments made pursuant to commercial activities.--Paragraph (1) does not apply with respect to any payment or transfer made pursuant to commercial activities in the regular course of a covered organization's business.

``(c) Certifications Regarding Disbursements for Campaign-Related Activity.--

``(1) Certification by chief executive officer.--If, at any time during a calendar quarter, a covered organization makes a disbursement of funds for campaign-related activity using funds described in subsection (a)(1), the chief executive officer of the covered organization or the chief executive officer's designee (or, if the organization does not have a chief executive officer, the highest ranking official of the organization or the highest ranking official's designee) shall file a statement with the Commission which contains the following certifications:

``(A) None of the campaign-related activity for which the organization disbursed the funds during the quarter was made in cooperation, consultation, or concert with, or at the request or suggestion of, any candidate or any authorized committee or agent of such candidate, or political committee of a political party or agent of any political party.

``(B) The chief executive officer or highest ranking official of the covered organization (as the case may be) has reviewed and approved each statement and report filed by the organization under section 304 with respect to any such disbursement made during the quarter.

``(C) Each statement and report filed by the organization under section 304 with respect to any such disbursement made during the quarter is complete and accurate.

``(D) All such disbursements made during the quarter are in compliance with this Act.

``(E) No portion of the amounts used to make any such disbursements during the quarter is attributable to funds received by the organization that were restricted by the person who provided the funds from being used for campaign-related activity pursuant to subsection (b).

``(2) Application of electronic filing rules.--Section

304(d)(1) shall apply with respect to a statement required under this subsection in the same manner as such section applies with respect to a statement under subsection (c) or (g) of section 304.

``(3) Deadline.--The chief executive officer or highest ranking official of a covered organization (as the case may be) shall file the statement required under this subsection with respect to a calendar quarter not later than 15 days after the end of the quarter.

``(d) Definitions.--For purposes of this section, the following definitions apply:

``(1) Covered organization.--The term `covered organization' means any of the following:

``(A) Any corporation which is subject to section 316(a).

``(B) Any labor organization (as defined in section 316).

``(C) Any organization described in paragraph (4), (5), or (6) of section 501(c) of the Internal Revenue Code of 1986 and exempt from tax under section 501(a) of such Code.

``(D) Any political organization under section 527 of the Internal Revenue Code of 1986, other than a political committee under this Act.

``(2) Campaign-related activity.--

``(A) In general.--The term `campaign-related activity' means--

``(i) an independent expenditure consisting of a public communication (as defined in section 301(22)), a transfer of funds to another person (other than the transferor itself) for the purpose of making such an independent expenditure by that person or by any other person, or (in accordance with subparagraph (B)) a transfer of funds to another person (other than the transferor itself) which is deemed to have been made for the purpose of making such an independent expenditure by that person or by any other person; or

``(ii) an electioneering communication, a transfer of funds to another person (other than the transferor itself) for the purpose of making an electioneering communication by that person or by any other person, or (in accordance with subparagraph (B)) a transfer of funds to another person (other than the transferor itself)which is deemed to have been made for the purpose of making an electioneering communication by that person or by any other person.

``(B) Rule for deeming transfers made for purpose of campaign-related activity.--For purposes of subparagraph (A), in determining whether a transfer of funds by one person to another person shall be deemed to have been made for the purpose of making an independent expenditure consisting of a public communication or an electioneering communication, the following rules apply:

``(i) The transfer shall be deemed to have been made for the purpose of making such an independent expenditure or an electioneering communication if--

``(I) the person designates, requests, or suggests that the amounts be used for such independent expenditures or electioneering communications and the person to whom the amounts were transferred agrees to do so or does so;

``(II) the person making such independent expenditures or electioneering communications or another person acting on that person's behalf expressly solicited the person for a donation or payment for making or paying for any such independent expenditure or electioneering communication;

``(III) the person and the person to whom the amounts were transferred engaged in substantial written or oral discussion regarding the person either making, or donating or paying for, such independent expenditures or electioneering communications;

``(IV) the person or the person to whom the amounts were transferred knew or had reason to know of the covered organization's intent to disburse funds for such independent expenditures or electioneering communications; or

``(V) the person or the person to whom the amounts were transferred made such an independent expenditure or electioneering communication during the 2-year period which ends on the date on which the amounts were transferred.

``(ii) The transfer shall not be deemed to have been made for the purpose of making such an independent expenditure or an electioneering communication if the transfer was a commercial transaction occurring in the ordinary course of business between the person and the person to whom the amounts were transferred, unless there is affirmative evidence that the amounts were transferred for the purpose of making such an independent expenditure or electioneering communication.

``(3) Unrestricted donor payment.--The term `unrestricted donor payment' means a payment to a covered organization which consists of a donation or payment from a person other than the covered organization, except that such term does not include--

``(A) any payment made pursuant to commercial activities in the regular course of a covered organization's business; or

``(B) any donation or payment which is designated by the person making the donation or payment to be used for campaign-related activity or made in response to a solicitation for funds to be used for campaign-related activity.".

Sec. 213. Optional Use of Separate Account by Covered Organizations for Campaign-Related Activity

Title III of the Federal Election Campaign Act of 1971 (2 U.S.C. 431 et seq.), as amended by section 212, is further amended by adding at the end the following new section:

``Sec. 326. Optional Use of Separate Account by Covered Organizations for Campaign-Related Activity

``(a) Optional Use of Separate Account.--

``(1) Establishment of account.--

``(A) In general.--At its option, a covered organization may make disbursements for campaign- related activity using amounts from a bank account established and controlled by the organization to be known as the Campaign-Related Activity Account (hereafter in this section referred to as the `Account'), which shall be maintained separately from all other accounts of the organization and which shall consist exclusively of the deposits described in paragraph (2).

``(B) Mandatory use of account after establishment.--

If a covered organization establishes an Account under this section, it may not make disbursements for campaign-related activity from any source other than amounts from the Account.

``(C) Exclusive use of account for campaign-related activity.--Amounts in the Account shall be used exclusively for disbursements by the covered organization for campaign-related activity. After such disbursements are made, information with respect to deposits made to the Account shall be disclosed in accordance with section 304(g)(5) or section 304(f)(6).

``(2) Deposits described.--The deposits described in this paragraph are deposits of the following amounts:

``(A) Amounts donated or paid to the covered organization by a person other than the organization for the purpose of being used for campaign-related activity, and for which the person providing the amounts has designated that the amounts be used for campaign-related activity with respect to a specific election or specific candidate.

``(B) Amounts donated or paid to the covered organization by a person other than the organization for the purpose of being used for campaign-related activity, and for which the person providing the amounts has not designated that the amounts be used for campaign-related activity with respect to a specific election or specific candidate.

``(C) Amounts donated or paid to the covered organization by a person other than the organization in response to a solicitation for funds to be used for campaign-related activity.

``(D) Amounts transferred to the Account by the covered organization from other accounts of the organization, including from the organization's general treasury funds.

``(3) No treatment as political committee.--The establishment and administration of an Account in accordance with this subsection shall not by itself be treated as the establishment or administration of a political committee for any purpose of this Act.

``(b) Reduction in Amounts Otherwise Available for Account in Response to Demand of General Donors.--

``(1) In general.--If a covered organization which has established an Account obtains any revenues during a year which are attributable to a donation or payment from a person other than the covered organization, and if any person who makes such a donation or payment to the organization notifies the organization in writing (at the time of making the donation or payment) that the organization may not use the donation or payment for campaign-related activity, the organization shall reduce the amount of its revenues available for deposits to the Account which are described in subsection (a)(3)(D) during the year by the amount of the donation or payment.

``(2) Exception.--Paragraph (1) does not apply with respect to any payment made pursuant to commercial activities in the regular course of a covered organization's business.

``(c) Covered Organization Defined.--In this section, the term `covered organization' means any of the following:

``(1) Any corporation which is subject to section 316(a).

``(2) Any labor organization (as defined in section 316).

``(3) Any organization described in paragraph (4), (5), or (6) of section 501(c) of the Internal Revenue Code of 1986 and exempt from tax under section 501(a) of such Code.

``(4) Any political organization under section 527 of the Internal Revenue Code of 1986, other than a political committee under this Act.

``(d) Campaign-Related Activity Defined.--In this section, the term `campaign-related activity' has the meaning given such term in section 325.''.

Sec. 214. Modification of Rules Relating to Disclaimer Statements Required for Certain Communications

(a) Applying Requirements to All Independent Expenditure Communications.--Section 318(a) of the Federal Election Campaign Act of 1971 (2 U.S.C. 441d(a)) is amended by striking ``for the purpose of financing communications expressly advocating the election or defeat of a clearly identified candidate'' and inserting ``for an independent expenditure consisting of a public communication''.

(b) Stand by Your Ad Requirements.--

(1) Maintenance of existing requirements for communications by political parties and other political committees.--Section 318(d)(2) of such Act (2 U.S.C. 441d(d)(2)) is amended—

(A) in the heading, by striking ``others'' and inserting ``political committees'';

(B) by striking ``subsection (a)'' and inserting ``subsection (a) which is paid for by a political committee (including a political committee of a political party), other than a political committee which makes only electioneering communications or independent expenditures consisting of public communications,''; and

(C) by striking ``or other person'' each place it appears.

(2) Special disclaimer requirements for certain communications.--Section 318 of such Act (2 U.S.C. 441d) is amended by adding at the end the following new subsection:

``(e) Communications by Others.--

``(1) In general.--Any communication described in paragraph (3) of subsection (a) which is transmitted through radio or television (other than a communication to which subsection (d)(2) applies because the communication is paid for by a political committee, including a political committee of a political party, other than a political committee which makes only electioneering communications or independent expenditures consisting of public communications) shall include, in addition to the requirements of that paragraph, the following:

``(A) The individual disclosure statement described in paragraph (2) (if the person paying for the communication is an individual) or the organizational disclosure statement described in paragraph (3) (if the person paying for the communication is not an individual).

``(B) If the communication is an electioneering communication or an independent expenditure consisting of a public communication and is paid for in whole or in part with a payment which is treated as a disbursement by a covered organization for campaign- related activity under section 325, the significant funder disclosure statement described in paragraph (4) (if applicable), unless, on the basis of criteria established in regulations promulgated by the Commission, the communication is of such short duration that including the statement in the communication would constitute a hardship to the person paying for the communication by requiring a disproportionate amount of the communication's content to consist of the statement.

``(C) If the communication is an electioneering communication or an independent expenditure consisting of a public communication and is paid for in whole or in part with a payment which is treated as a disbursement by a covered organization for campaign- related activity under section 325, the Top Five Funders list described in paragraph (5) (if applicable), unless, on the basis of criteria established in regulations promulgated by the Commission, the communication is of such short duration that including the Top Five Funders list in the communication would constitute a hardship to the person paying for the communication by requiring a disproportionate amount of the communication's content to consist of the Top Five Funders list.

``(2) Individual disclosure statement described.--The individual disclosure statement described in this paragraph is the following: `I am _______, and I approve this message.', with the blank filled in with the name of the applicable individual.

``(3) Organizational disclosure statement described.--The organizational disclosure statement described in this paragraph is the following: `I am _______, the _______ of _______, and _______ approves this message.', with--

``(A) the first blank to be filled in with the name of the applicable individual;

``(B) the second blank to be filled in with the title of the applicable individual; and

``(C) the third and fourth blank each to be filled in with the name of the organization or other person paying for the communication.

``(4) Significant funder disclosure statement described.--

``(A) Statement if significant funder is an individual.--If the significant funder of a communication paid for in whole or in part with a payment which is treated as a disbursement by a covered organization for campaign-related activity under section 325 is an individual, the significant funder disclosure statement described in this paragraph is the following: `I am _______. I helped to pay for this message, and I approve it.', with the blank filled in with the name of the applicable individual.

``(B) Statement if significant funder is not an individual.--If the significant funder of a communication paid for in whole or in part with a payment which is treated as a disbursement by a covered organization for campaign-related activity under section 325 is not an individual, the significant funder disclosure statement described in this paragraph is the following: `I am _______, the _______ of _______. _______ helped to pay for this message, and _______ approves it.', with--

``(i) the first blank to be filled in with the name of the applicable individual;

``(ii) the second blank to be filled in with the title of the applicable individual; and

``(iii) the third, fourth, and fifth blank each to be filled in with the name of the significant funder of the communication.

``(C) Significant funder defined.--

``(i) Independent expenditures.--For purposes of this paragraph, the `significant funder' with respect to an independent expenditure consisting of a public communication paid for in whole or in part with a payment which is treated as a disbursement by a covered organization for campaign-related activity under section 325 shall be determined as follows:

``(I) If any report filed by any organization with respect to the independent expenditure under section 304 includes information on any person who made a payment to the organization in an amount equal to or exceeding $100,000 which was designated by the person to be used for campaign-related activity consisting of that specific independent expenditure (as required to be included in the report under section 304(g)(5)(A)(i)), the person who is identified among all such reports as making the largest such payment.

``(II) If any report filed by any organization with respect to the independent expenditure under section 304 includes information on any person who made a payment to the organization in an amount equal to or exceeding $100,000 which was designated by the person to be used for campaign-related activity with respect to the same election or in support of the same candidate (as required to be included in the report under section 304(g)(5)(A)(i)) but subclause (I) does not apply, the person who is identified among all such reports as making the largest such payment.

``(III) If any report filed by any organization with respect to the independent expenditure under section 304 includes information on any person who made a payment to the organization which was provided for the purpose of being used for campaign-related activity or in response to a solicitation for funds to be used for campaign-related activity (as required to be included in the report under section 304(g)(5)(A)(i)) but subclause (I) or subclause (II) does not apply, the person who is identified among all such reports as making the largest such payment.

``(IV) If none of the reports filed by any organization with respect to the independent expenditure under section 304 includes information on any person (other than the organization) who made a payment to the organization which was provided for the purpose of being used for campaign-related activity or in response to a solicitation for funds to be used for campaign-related activity, but any of such reports includes information on any person who made an unrestricted donor payment to the organization (as required to be included in the report under section 304(g)(5)(A)(ii)), the person who is identified among all such reports as making the largest such unrestricted donor payment.

``(ii) Electioneering communications.--For purposes of this paragraph, the `significant funder' with respect to an electioneering communication paid for in whole or in part with a payment which is treated as a disbursement by a covered organization for campaign-related activity under section 325, shall be determined as follows:

``(I) If any report filed by any organization with respect to the electioneering communication under section 304 includes information on any person who made a payment to the organization in an amount equal to or exceeding $100,000 which was designated by the person to be used for campaign- related activity consisting of that specific electioneering communication (as required to be included in the report under section 304(f)(6)(A)(i)), the person who is identified among all such reports as making the largest such payment.

``(II) If any report filed by any organization with respect to the electioneering communication under section 304 includes information on any person who made a payment to the organization in an amount equal to or exceeding $100,000 which was designated by the person to be used for campaign- related activity with respect to the same election or in support of the same candidate (as required to be included in the report under section 304(f)(6)(A)(i)) but subclause (I) does not apply, the person who is identified among all such reports as making the largest such payment.

``(III) If any report filed by any organization with respect to the electioneering communication under section 304 includes information on any person who made a payment to the organization which was provided for the purpose of being used for campaign- related activity or in response to a solicitation for funds to be used for campaign-related activity (as required to be included in the report under section 304(f)(6)(A)(i)) but subclause (I) or subclause (II) does not apply, the person who is identified among all such reports as making the largest such payment.

``(IV) If none of the reports filed by any organization with respect to the electioneering communication under section 304 includes information on any person who made a payment to the organization which was provided for the purpose of being used for campaign- related activity or in response to a solicitation for funds to be used for campaign-related activity, but any of such reports includes information on any person who made an unrestricted donor payment to the organization (as required to be included in the report under section 304(f)(6)(A)(ii)), the person who is identified among all such reports as making the largest such unrestricted donor payment.

``(5) Top 5 funders list described.--With respect to a communication paid for in whole or in part with a payment which is treated as a disbursement by a covered organization for campaign-related activity under section 325, the Top 5 Funders list described in this paragraph is--

``(A) in the case of a disbursement for an independent expenditure consisting of a public communication, a list of the 5 persons (or, in the case of a communication transmitted through radio, the 2 persons) who provided the largest payments of any type which are required under section 304(g)(5)(A) to be included in the reports filed by any organization with respect to that independent expenditure under section 304, together with the amount of the payments each such person provided; or

``(B) in the case of a disbursement for an electioneering communication, a list of the 5 persons (or, in the case of a communication transmitted through radio, the 2 persons) who provided the largest payments of any type which are required under section 304(f)(6)(A) to be included in the reports filed by any organization with respect to that electioneering communication under section 304, together with the amount of the payments each such person provided.

``(6) Method of conveyance of statement.--

``(A) Communications transmitted through radio.--In the case of a communication to which this subsection applies which is transmitted through radio, the disclosure statements required under paragraph (1) shall be made by audio by the applicable individual in a clearly spoken manner.

``(B) Communications transmitted through television.--In the case of a communication to which this subsection applies which is transmitted through television, the information required under paragraph (1)--

``(i) shall appear in writing at the end of the communication in a clearly readable manner, with a reasonable degree of color contrast between the background and the printed statement, for a period of at least 6 seconds; and

``(ii) except in the case of a Top 5 Funders list described in paragraph (5), shall also be conveyed by an unobscured, full-screen view of the applicable individual, or by the applicable individual making the statement in voice-over accompanied by a clearly identifiable photograph or similar image of the individual.

``(7) Applicable individual defined.--In this subsection, the term `applicable individual' means, with respect to a communication to which this paragraph applies--

``(A) if the communication is paid for by an individual or if the significant funder of the communication under paragraph (4) is an individual, the individual involved;

``(B) if the communication is paid for by a corporation or if the significant funder of the communication under paragraph (4) is a corporation, the chief executive officer of the corporation (or, if the corporation does not have a chief executive officer, the highest ranking official of the corporation);

``(C) if the communication is paid for by a labor organization or if the significant funder of the communication under paragraph (4) is a labor organization, the highest ranking officer of the labor organization; or

``(D) if the communication is paid for by any other person or if the significant funder of the communication under paragraph (4) is any other person, the highest ranking official of such person.

``(8) Covered organization defined.--In this subsection, the term `covered organization' means any of the following:

``(A) Any corporation which is subject to section 316(a).

``(B) Any labor organization (as defined in section 316).

``(C) Any organization described in paragraph (4), (5), or (6) of section 501(c) of the Internal Revenue Code of 1986 and exempt from tax under section 501(a) of such Code.

``(D) Any political organization under section 527 of the Internal Revenue Code of 1986, other than a political committee under this Act.

``(9) Other definitions.--In this subsection, the terms `campaign-related activity' and `unrestricted donor payment' have the meaning given such terms in section 325.''.

(3) Application to certain mass mailings.--Section 318(a)(3) of such Act (2 U.S.C. 441d(a)(3)) is amended to read as follows:

``(3) if not authorized by a candidate, an authorized political committee of a candidate, or its agents, shall clearly state--

``(A) the name and permanent street address, telephone number, or World Wide Web address of the person who paid for the communication;

``(B) if the communication is an independent expenditure consisting of a mass mailing (as defined in section 301(23)) which is paid for in whole or in part with a payment which is treated as a disbursement by a covered organization for campaign-related activity under section 325, the name and permanent street address, telephone number, or World Wide Web address of--

``(i) the significant funder of the communication, if any (as determined in accordance with subsection (e)(4)(C)(i)); and

``(ii) each person who would be included in the Top 5 Funders list which would be submitted with respect to the communication if the communication were transmitted through television, if any (as determined in accordance with subsection (e)(5)); and

``(C) that the communication is not authorized by any candidate or candidate's committee.''.

(4) Application to political robocalls.--Section 318 of such Act (2 U.S.C. 441d), as amended by paragraph (2), is further amended by adding at the end the following new subsection:

``(f) Special Rules for Political Robocalls.--

``(1) Requiring communications to include certain disclaimer statements.--Any communication consisting of a political robocall which would be subject to the requirements of subsection (e) if the communication were transmitted through radio or television shall include the following:

``(A) The individual disclosure statement described in subsection (e)(2) (if the person paying for the communication is an individual) or the organizational disclosure statement described in subsection (e)(3) (if the person paying for the communication is not an individual).

``(B) If the communication is an electioneering communication or an independent expenditure consisting of a public communication and is paid for in whole or in part with a payment which is treated as a disbursement by a covered organization for campaign- related activity under section 325, the significant funder disclosure statement described in subsection (e)(4) (if applicable).

``(2) Timing of certain statement.--The statement required to be included under paragraph (1)(A) shall be made at the beginning of the political robocall.

``(3) Political robocall defined.--In this subsection, the term `political robocall' means any outbound telephone call--

``(A) in which a person is not available to speak with the person answering the call, and the call instead plays a recorded message; and

``(B) which promotes, supports, attacks, or opposes a candidate for election for Federal office.''.

Subtitle C--Reporting Requirements for Registered Lobbyists

Sec. 221. Requiring Registered Lobbyists to Report Information on Independent Expenditures and Electioneering Communications

(a) In General.--Section 5(d)(1) of the Lobbying Disclosure Act of 1995 (2 U.S.C. 1604(d)(1)) is amended--

(1) by striking ``and'' at the end of subparagraph (F);

(2) by redesignating subparagraph (G) as subparagraph (I);

and

(3) by inserting after subparagraph (F) the following new subparagraphs:

``(G) the amount of any independent expenditure (as defined in section 301(17) of the Federal Election Campaign Act of 1971 (2 U.S.C. 431(17)) equal to or greater than $1,000 made by such person or organization, and for each such expenditure the name of each candidate being supported or opposed and the amount spent supporting or opposing each such candidate;

``(H) the amount of any electioneering communication (as defined in section 304(f)(3) of such Act (2 U.S.C. 434(f)(3)) equal to or greater than $1,000 made by such person or organization, and for each such communication the name of the candidate referred to in the communication and whether the communication involved was in support of or in opposition to the candidate;

and''.

(b) Effective Date.--The amendments made by this section shall apply with respect to reports for semiannual periods described in section 5(d)(1) of the Lobbying Disclosure Act of 1995 that begin after the date of the enactment of this Act.

Title III--Disclosure by Covered Organizations of Information on Campaign-Related Activity

Sec. 301. Requiring Disclosure by Covered Organizations of Information on Campaign-Related Activity

Title III of the Federal Election Campaign Act of 1971 (2 U.S.C. 431 et seq.), as amended by section 213, is amended by adding at the end the following new section:

``Sec. 327. Disclosures by Covered Organizations to Shareholders, Members, and Donors of Information on Disbursements for Campaign-Related Activity

``(a) Including Information in Regular Periodic Reports.--

``(1) In general.--A covered organization which submits regular, periodic reports to its shareholders, members, or donors on its finances or activities shall include in each such report the information described in paragraph (2) with respect to the disbursements made by the organization for campaign- related activity during the period covered by the report.

``(2) Information described.--The information described in this paragraph is, for each disbursement for campaign-related activity--

``(A) the date of the independent expenditure or electioneering communication involved;

``(B) the amount of the independent expenditure or electioneering communication involved;

``(C) the name of the candidate identified in the independent expenditure or electioneering communication involved, the office sought by the candidate, and (if applicable) whether the independent expenditure or electioneering communication involved was in support of or in opposition to the candidate;

``(D) in the case of a transfer of funds to another person, the information required by subparagraphs (A) through (C), as well as the name of the recipient of the funds and the date and amount of the funds transferred;

``(E) the source of such funds; and

``(F) such other information as the Commission
determines is appropriate to further the purposes of this subsection.

``(b) Hyperlink to Information Included in Reports Filed With Commission.--

``(1) Requiring posting of hyperlink.--If a covered
organization maintains an Internet site, the organization shall post on such Internet site a hyperlink from its homepage to the location on the Internet site of the Commission which contains the following information:

``(A) The information the organization is required to report under section 304(g)(5)(A) with respect to public independent expenditures.

``(B) The information the organization is required to include in a statement of disbursements for electioneering communications under section 304(f)(6).

``(2) Deadline; duration of posting.--The covered organization shall post the hyperlink described in paragraph (1) not later than 24 hours after the Commission posts the information described in such paragraph on the Internet site of the Commission, and shall ensure that the hyperlink remains on the Internet site of the covered organization until the expiration of the 1-year period which begins on the date of the election with respect to which the public independent expenditures or electioneering communications are made.

``(c) Covered Organization Defined.--In this section, the term `covered organization' means any of the following:

``(1) Any corporation which is subject to section 316(a).

``(2) Any labor organization (as defined in section 316).

``(3) Any organization described in paragraph (4), (5), or (6) of section 501(c) of the Internal Revenue Code of 1986 and exempt from tax under section 501(a) of such Code.

``(4) Any political organization under section 527 of the Internal Revenue Code of 1986, other than a political committee under this Act.''.

TITLE IV--OTHER PROVISIONS

Sec. 401. Judicial Review

(a) Special Rules for Actions Brought on Constitutional Grounds.--If any action is brought for declaratory or injunctive relief to challenge the constitutionality of any provision of this Act or any amendment made by this Act, the following rules shall apply:

(1) The action shall be filed in the United States District Court for the District of Columbia, and an appeal from a decision of the District Court may be taken to the Court of Appeals for the District of Columbia Circuit.

(2) A copy of the complaint shall be delivered promptly to the Clerk of the House of Representatives and the Secretary of the Senate.

(3) It shall be the duty of the United States District Court for the District of Columbia, the Court of Appeals for the District of Columbia Circuit, and the Supreme Court of the United States to advance on the docket and to expedite to the greatest possible extent the disposition of the action and appeal.

(b) Intervention by Members of Congress.--In any action in which the constitutionality of any provision of this Act or any amendment made by this Act is raised, any member of the House of Representatives (including a Delegate or Resident Commissioner to the Congress) or Senate shall have the right to intervene either in support of or opposition to the position of a party to the case regarding the constitutionality of the provision or amendment. To avoid duplication of efforts and reduce the burdens placed on the parties to the action, the court in any such action may make such orders as it considers necessary, including orders to require intervenors taking similar positions to file joint papers or to be represented by a single attorney at oral argument.

(c) Challenge by Members of Congress.--Any Member of the House of Representatives (including a Delegate or Resident Commissioner to the Congress) or Senate may bring an action, subject to the special rules described in subsection (a), for declaratory or injunctive relief to challenge the constitutionality of any provision of this Act or any amendment made by this Act.

Sec. 402. Severability

If any provision of this Act or amendment made by this Act, or the application of a provision or amendment to any person or circumstance, is held to be unconstitutional, the remainder of this Act and amendments made by this Act, and the application of the provisions and amendment to any person or circumstance, shall not be affected by the holding.

Sec. 403. Effective Date

Except as otherwise provided, this Act and the amendments made by this Act shall take effect upon the expiration of the 30-day period which begins on the date of the enactment of this Act, and shall take effect without regard to whether or not the Federal Election Commission has promulgated regulations to carry out such amendments.

Purpose of the Legislation

INTRODUCTION

As a result of the United States Supreme Court's ruling in Citizens United vs. FEC, corporations and unions may for the first time in recent memory spend unlimited sums from their treasuries to influence federal elections. These funds will often be routed through other organizations, enabling the true funders to avoid disclosure. Unless action is taken, the public will be left in the dark to wonder whose interests are truly being served by the flood of negative advertising that will likely come to dominate campaigns. Voters will be unable to adequately evaluate the interests that support particular candidates, and will be impaired in placing candidates along the political spectrum. Candidates will not be able to discover who is behind these ads, leaving them unable to adequately disavow a purported supporter with whom the candidate disagrees. An environment will be created where disingenuous and untruthful advertising campaigns will be rewarded.

To prosper, our democracy requires transparency and accountability in our political campaigns. The Committee believes that knowing the source of political spending allows voters to better assess the truthfulness and accuracy of the claims of the spenders and the candidates. It invites a healthy skepticism and allows voters to investigate the motives of the sponsor. By an 8-1 majority, the Supreme Court has strongly reaffirmed the constitutionality and necessity of laws that require the disclosure of political spending. Without the disinfectant of disclosure, the virus of deceitful campaigns will only spread.

H.R. 5175, the Democracy is Strengthened by Casting Light on Spending in Elections Act (DISCLOSE Act), allows voters to follow the money, by requiring all covered organizations to report to the FEC within 24 hours their campaign-related activity and their transfers of money to other groups which are then available for campaign-related activity. Disclosing these transfers of money will ensure that special-interest money cannot hide behind sham organizations and shell corporations.

If outside groups spend their funds in campaigns, voters have a right to know who is delivering and paying for the message.

Under this bill, heads of organizations will be required to `stand by their ad' in the same way candidates must. The top funder of the ad must also `stand by their ad' and the top five contributors will be listed on the screen at the end of the ad.

H.R. 5175 assures transparency and enhances accountability.

The bill applies alike to corporations, labor unions, trade associations and non-profit advocacy organizations. H.R. 5175 provides prompt and honest disclosure of political spending by all those seeking to influence our elections.

The Committee is also concerned that the Citizens United decision may have the effect of opening the door to foreign nationals influencing our elections. From the inception of the Republic, Congress has been concerned with foreign governments and interests trying to exert influence on our elections. The Court's decision invites those interests to use corporations over which they have control to influence American elections.

H.R. 5175 seeks to diminish the ability of corporations to circumvent existing law.

The Committee is further concerned that large government contractors will use their financial muscle to maintain or gain unwarranted advantage in the procurement process. The Committee believes that corporate political spending could undermine the integrity of government contracting decisions, resulting in the perpetuation of unnecessary and wasteful projects. The Committee is concerned that small businesses seeking government contracts will be put at a substantial disadvantage.

The public is likewise concerned with the potential consequences of the Citizens United decision. Indeed, the Committee received nearly 2,500 emails and roughly 4,500 phone calls in one week from the concerned citizens who urged Congress to consider legislation that addresses the loopholes created by the Citizens United ruling. The Committee believes that the DISCLOSE Act reflects the will of the American people.

In sum, H.R. 5175 promotes openness in our politics. The legislation has bipartisan and popular support. The bill preparation has been exceptionally transparent, including releasing an outline of the bill well in advance of drafting, working with a bipartisan team to craft a bill based on that framework, and holding multiple hearings after releasing the actual bill for review. This early announcement of the bill's framework was intended to facilitate an open and healthy discussion. Six Congressional hearings, amongst numerous Committees of jurisdiction, were held on the Citizens United decision and the proper Congressional response. Members of both parties were invited to and did work on drafting a bill based on the framework. The DISCLOSE Act has been crafted in the open in the same spirit of openness that it strives to achieve for the campaign finance system.

Compelling Need for Additional Disclosure in Light of Citizens United

The vast amount of money that the Citizens United decision makes available for use in influencing federal elections dwarfs what had previously been available. Candidates, who must operate under contribution limits designed to protect them from undue influence, are put at a great disadvantage. The Committee believes that legislative action is necessary to protect our electoral system against the dangers posed when vast corporate wealth can be unleashed anonymously to advance the interests of corporate managers, at the expense of shareholders and the public.

The Committee is concerned about the potential risk that some corporate managers will misuse corporate funds to pursue their own personal and political objectives. This risk is not currently addressed in existing corporate governance mechanisms, state law, SEC regulations, or stock exchange rules.[1] There are no rules that require corporate managers or company boards of directors to inform shareholders of decisions to spend corporate treasury money on elections. Corporations can now flood the campaign finance system secretly, without any disclosure or possibility of a private corporate governance response to correct this misuse. Indeed, these dangers have already begun to materialize, with business associations, unions, and other outside groups taking advantage of Citizens United to ``pour money'' into primary elections across the country--without disclosure of the major funding sources behind political ads.[2]

During the last election cycle, the Fortune 100 companies alone had combined revenues of $13.1 trillion and profits of $605 billion.[3] In comparison, the 2,382 House and Senate candidates seeking office in 2008 spent a total of $1.38 billion.[4]

Total spending on federal elections in 2008 was more than $5.3 billion from political parties, outside groups, candidates, and PACs.[5] One oil company alone made over $45 billion dollars in profit in 2008, nine times the total amount spent on all federal elections.

The Committee is concerned that these vast corporate resources, coupled with the lack of transparency and accountability in their use, will deny voters important information that they need to assess candidates and make decisions.[6] Unidentified interests will determine the shape and course of campaigns. Those special interests will be able to do so without ever having to reveal themselves or subject their motives to public scrutiny.

The efforts by corporations, unions, interest groups, and individuals to evade campaign finance restrictions or to hide or obfuscate their identities when making political expenditures are well-documented.[7] It is now possible for corporations to donate anonymously to nonprofit civic leagues and trade associations.[8] Under the current rules for outside groups, any entity, including a corporation or labor union, that directly spends money on electioneering communications or independent expenditure campaigns must report those expenditures to the Federal Election Commission (FEC), which discloses them to the public. But when that spending is done anonymously through an often complex, multi-layered series of transactions with nonprofit civic leagues and trade associations--many of which use vacuous or even misleading names--it allows the true spender behind a message to evade disclosure requirements and mislead voters.[9] Citizens United exacerbates these problems, allowing nonprofit groups and associations that are not required to disclose their donors to use unlimited corporate or labor contributions to buy political commercials.

History has also provided ample cause for concern about these matters. The record assembled in McConnell v. FEC is rife with examples of corporate efforts to mask their identities and circumvent then-existing campaign finance laws in attempts to influence federal elections.[10] Evidence was presented, for example, about a group called The Coalition--Americans Working for Real Change (``The Coalition'').[11] The Coalition, which was funded by business interests and ran ads in the 1996 election cycle that were paid for with corporate general treasury funds, ``was able to avoid FECA's disclosure requirements and hide its corporate sponsors behind an ambiguous and unobjectionable pseudonym.''[12]

Evidence was also presented about Citizens for Better Medicare (``CBM"), a group funded by the pharmaceutical industry. Judge Kollar-Kotelly found that CBM ``spent heavily on candidate-centered issue advertisements designed to influence the 2000 general election and paid for with the general treasury funds of their corporate members, thereby avoiding the source limitations of FECA."[13] As with The Coalition, CBM ``also used issue advocacy to avoid FECA's disclosure requirements."[14]

The district court in McConnell found these and other incidents detailed in its extensive record to be far from isolated, as it noted in its per curiam opinion that freedom from disclosure provisions ``permitted various interest groups to conceal the true identity of the source behind the advertisement."[15] Thus, the Court added, ``following both the 1996 and 2000 elections, corporations and unions used their general treasury funds to run advertisements apparently aimed at influencing federal elections and avoiding FECA's longstanding disclosure provisions.'[16]

Many scholarly studies and expert reports support these findings. The Annenberg Public Policy Center, for example, in Issue Advertising in the 1999-2000 Election Cycle, found that

``[i]ssue advocacy masks the identity of some key players and by so doing, it deprives citizens of information about sources of messages which research tells us is a vital part of assessing message credibility."[17] It also found that, ``[o]ver the last three election cycles, the number of groups sponsoring ads has exploded, and consumers often don't know who these groups are, who funds them, and whom they represent."[18] Along similar lines, the Krasno & Sorauf expert report cited in the per curiam McConnell opinion noted that the public has difficulty identifying those responsible for issue advertisements that identify candidates.[19]

Finally, testimony from various sources in the McConnell case supports the judges'--and our--views that corporations had been both circumventing disclosure obligations and obfuscating their identities. For example, political consultant Terry S. Beckett testified that

> [t]he Republican Leadership Council (``RLC") also ran so-called ``issue-ads" on television in the 2000 Congressional campaign . . . . [Two of t]hese ads accuse [Republican Candidate Ric] Keller of acting ``like a liberal." I found it [ ] ironic, not to mention unsettling, to learn of reports that the hundreds of thousands of dollars the RLC spent on these ads trying to defeat Mr. Keller were actually provided by the Florida sugar industry . . . . And the fact that I, a general consultant in this same race with long high-level experience in Florida politics, was not aware until earlier this year of whose money was behind these ads strongly underlines the need for disclosure of this kind of stealth electioneering financed with corporate funds.[20]

In sum, the Committee is cognizant of the long history of circumvention of disclosure rules, and is particularly attuned to relatively recent efforts by corporations, as described in the McConnell opinion and evidenced in the McConnell litigation record as well as other sources, to evade disclosure rules and hide their identities. Given the new flood of corporate treasury funds likely to be spent on elections in the wake of Citizens United, efforts to devise ways to circumvent disclosure rules are likely to increase. This, together with evasion of current rules, makes it necessary to put in place the enhanced disclosure requirements in this legislation.

H.R. 5175 Provides for Effective Disclosure

The bill makes numerous reporting improvements in the current reporting system. All campaign-related expenditures made by a corporation, union, section 501(c)(4), or (6) organization, or section 527 organization must be disclosed on the organization's website with a clear link on the homepage within 24 hours of reporting such expenditures to the FEC.

Additionally, all campaign-related expenditures made by a corporation, union, section 501(c)(4), or (6) organization, or section 527 organization must be disclosed to shareholders and members of the organization in any financial reports the organization already provides on a periodic and/or annual basis to its shareholders or members.

The enhanced disclosure requirements of H.R. 5175 are needed to ensure that ``corporations live up to their civic responsibility by providing disclosure to the public through disclaimers and the Internet, directly to their stockholders or members, and to the Federal Election Commission."[21] The bill increases transparency for the public as to who is financing independent campaign ads and fills in many of the holes of the existing system, specifically as it relates to the practice of funneling campaign money through agents and conduits.[22]

Moreover, various factors--including the advent of the Internet, where particular communications can be circulated and remain available for viewing long after they are first broadcast, and the increasing frequency of political campaigns that effectively begin long before election day--have rendered the existing system of disclosure and disclaimer requirements (including the limited time periods during which some of those requirements currently apply) inadequate to protect fully the government's interest in ensuring that the electorate is fully informed about the sources of election-related spending, and that shareholders and citizens alike have the information they need to hold corporations and elected officials accountable for their positions and supporters.

H.R. 5175 is likewise an important corrective to the new corporate governance and electoral risks created by Citizens United. Requiring real-time, ongoing disclosure of election expenditures, allows shareholders and the public to monitor the use of corporations' capital in the election context, and take whatever actions they want to discipline such corporations if they are found to misuse their funds.[23] An effective disclosure regime must provide the information critical for voter comprehension in an easy to understand and timely fashion.[24] A survey of corporate directors reveals that the majority agree with the need for disclosure and transparency and do not believe that additional reporting requirements for corporate political spending would be too burdensome and costly.[25] The DISCLOSE Act recognizes that American voters are at minimum entitled to full and accurate reporting of campaign spending so that voters may know who is truly behind an attempt to influence their vote. Moreover, the Committee recognizes that modern campaigns have increased in length, such that earlier disclosure is necessary.[26]

The Supreme Court has consistently endorsed the principle that the public has the right to know about expenditures being made to influence election campaigns, and about the sources that are providing the funds used for such expenditures.[27] In Citizens United, the Supreme Court strongly reaffirmed the constitutionality of laws that require the disclosure of the money spent by such corporations to influence federal elections. An 8-1 majority of the U.S. Supreme Court explicitly stated that the type of disclosure in H.R. 5175 is ``not only constitutional, but is the expected and indeed necessary counter-balance to the new corporate right to expend unlimited funds in U.S. elections."[28] In his majority opinion, Justice Kennedy wrote, ``The First Amendment protects political speech; and disclosure permits citizens and shareholders to react to the speech of corporate entities in a proper way."[29]

H.R. 5175 Improves Disclaimer Requirements

The pervasive nature of campaign advertising means that most Americans, even those who might not be otherwise engaged in the political process, will come into contact with campaign advertising. Moreover, the lengthy nature of most modern campaigns means that many Americans will be exposed to campaign advertising for an extended period prior to the actual election. Many of these Americans may lack ready access to the information provided through the disclosure requirements. For this reason, disclaimers on the advertising itself are particularly important in improving the knowledge of the American people about who is funding independent expenditures and electioneering communications to influence Federal elections. Effective disclaimers enable the American people to assess advertisements as they see or hear them, making them aware of the sources of funding behind advertisements, and enabling them to use that information to help evaluate the persuasiveness of the advertisements. Effective disclaimers can also alert the electorate to connections between different advertisements, such as when different advertisements are supported by the same funding source. It is thus particularly important that disclaimers on all advertising be presented in a manner that can be quickly and easily understood, and is likely to be observed and retained, by those seeing or hearing the advertisement.

H.R. 5175 enhances disclaimers to identify sponsors of advertisements in a variety of mediums--broadcast television advertising, radio advertising, political robo-calls, and mass mailings. Leaders of corporations, unions, and organizations are required to identify that they are behind political ads. If any covered organization (corporation, union, section 501(c)(4), or (6) organization, or section 527 organization) makes disbursements for an independent expenditure or electioneering communication, the CEO or highest ranking official of that organization will be required to appear on camera to say that he or she ``approves this message," just like candidates have to do now.

H.R. 5175 requires the CEO of a corporation or head of any other covered organization to personally appear in the organization's independent expenditure or electioneering communication TV ads and take responsibility for the ad by stating that the corporation or other organization approves the message. The same statement must be read by the CEO or head of the organization in radio advertising. This stand-by-your-ad provision is similar to the stand-by-your-ad requirement that applies to federal candidates under current law. In addition, the legislation requires the top funder of a TV or radio ad also to appear in the ad and take responsibility for it. Academic literature demonstrates that information about those behind political ads is crucial for informed voter decision-making and that oral or audio disclaimers substantially improve listener comprehension.[30]

Additionally, for independent expenditure or electioneering communication ads that appear on TV, a covered organization must also list the top 5 funders who provided the largest payments to the covered organization that are available to be used to pay for the ads.

This listing helps the public, at the time they see the ad, to obtain information about the sponsors and funders of an ad, which helps them evaluate the ad to ``make informed decisions'' because they are now able to ``give proper weight to different speakers and messages.''[31]

In Citizens United, the Supreme Court upheld the disclaimer provisions in H.R. 5175 on grounds similar to the reasons it cited in support of disclosure requirements. The Court noted that disclaimer requirements, like disclosure, ``impose no ceiling'' on campaign-related activities, and ``do not prevent anyone from speaking.''[32] Instead, they provide the electorate with information, and ensure that the voters are fully informed about the person or group who is speaking. ``At the very least, the disclaimers avoid confusion by making clear that the ads are not funded by a candidate or political party.''[33]

H.R. 5175 Protects Taxpayer Dollars from Misuse

Under current law, government contractors are barred from making contributions to federal candidates.[34] Under existing FEC regulations, they are also barred from making expenditures to influence federal elections.[35] The reason for these longstanding laws is that federal contractors have a direct contractual relationship with the federal government and a heightened financial interest in government contracting decisions. The government has a compelling interest in ensuring that federal contractors, including corporations, do not use the power of their treasuries to buy favoritism in the federal contracting process.

There should be no pay-to-play in the award of government contracts. Campaign contributions from and expenditures by companies applying for and receiving government contracts and TARP funds should be limited to ensure that the American people can have faith in the fairness of how those funds are awarded.

Objective contracting criteria, and not special access, influence, or ingratiation resulting from political expenditures--or outright quid pro quo corruption--should determine how taxpayer dollars are spent. By the same token, contractors are in a position where they are vulnerable to government officials who might directly or indirectly pressure them to make expenditures in order to receive or keep contracts vital to their business. The integrity of the government contracting process has long been, and should continue to be, protected from coercion.

A wide range of government officials, including officials without any official role in the contracting process, have the ability to influence the award of government contracts through their informal relationships with fellow officials and other means. Further, the public perceives that this wide range of officials, including those without any official role in the contracting process, have the ability to influence the award of government contracts. To ensure that the restriction on independent expenditures and electioneering communications achieves its objectives, the Committee believes it is necessary for it to extend to all political parties, committees, and candidates for Federal office.

Like government contracts, financial assistance under title I of the Emergency Economic Stabilization Act of 2008 must be awarded, and must be perceived to be awarded and have been awarded, based on specific statutory criteria, and not based on other forms of inappropriate or corrupting influence. For the reasons explained above and in the bill's findings, the Committee believes it is necessary to extend the prohibition on independent expenditures and electioneering communications to recipients of funds under title I of the Emergency Economic Stabilization Act of 2008.

Accordingly, the DISCLOSE Act provides that contractors who have contracts with a value of $7 million or more are prohibited from making independent expenditures or electioneering communications in federal elections. This threshold was chosen to reflect the standard generally applied by the Small Business Administration to determine small business status. The same restrictions apply to recipients of TARP funds until such funds have been paid back. These requirements build on existing law and regulations, which have long prohibited contributions and expenditures by government contractors, whether contractors are corporations or not. Government contractors have been permitted, and will continue to be permitted, to make expenditures from a federal PAC.

H.R. 5175 PREVENTS FOREIGN INFLUENCE IN U.S. ELECTIONS

The danger of foreign interference in American affairs, and the power and duty of the Congress to guard against it, have been recognized since the very beginning of our Nation's history.[36] Over the years, foreign interests have demonstrated a specific desire and capacity to exert influence over United States elections and elections officials through political expenditures and electioneering. In 1966, Congress amended the Foreign Agents Registration Act to require complete public disclosure by persons acting for or in the interests of foreign principals--and to ban them from making political contributions--after hearing evidence of ``persistent efforts'' by foreign persons and concerns to influence American policy and elections.[37] In the 1990s, a Senate Committee found significant evidence that political contributions were being made at the secret direction of the Chinese government.[38] More recently, courts have also faced instances of attempts at foreign intrusion in federal elections.[39] These are but a few examples.

Well-settled law therefore already prohibits foreign nationals, whether citizens, businesses or governments, from voting in American elections and making political contributions and expenditures.[40] Although the Court in Citizens United left open the question ``whether the Government has a compelling interest in preventing foreign individuals or associations from influencing our Nation's political process,''[41] its decision has the practical effect of making such foreign influence possible. Current law defines foreign nationals to include foreign corporations--those organized under the law of a foreign country or with a principal place of business in a foreign country--but does not include domestic U.S. corporations that are owned or controlled by foreign nationals.[42] Until Citizens United was decided, all corporations were barred from making campaign contributions or expenditures, and it was therefore unnecessary for Congress to address the distinct concerns raised by foreign-owned or -controlled U.S. corporations. The effect of Citizens United, however, is that, while foreign nationals are banned from making contributions or expenditures to influence U.S. elections, domestic subsidiaries or affiliates controlled by these very same foreign corporations can make unrestrained expenditures to influence the outcome of elections or the decisions of elected officials.[43]

The risk to our political process posed by foreign influence is not merely theoretical. According to Internal Revenue Service data, as of 2005 there were roughly 62,000 corporations with at least one 25+% foreign owner,[44] and these companies' control over all corporate assets had risen dramatically, from just 1.3% in 1971 to roughly 13.9% in 2005.[45] It is now common for foreign corporations to own U.S. corporations in whole or in part, as in the case of Anheuser-Busch (Belgian parent), 7-Eleven (Japanese parent), Ben & Jerry's (British parent), and T-Mobile USA (German parent).[46]

United States corporate equity and debt are also held by foreign individuals and sovereign wealth funds: China Investment Corporation (9% stake in Morgan Stanley); Abu Dhabi Investment Authority (4.9% stake in Citigroup); and Kingdom Holding, a company run by a member of the Saudi royal family (4.3% stake in Citigroup).[47] United States companies are even owned or controlled by foreign nationals themselves: CITGO (owned by Petroleos de Venezuela S.A., controlled by President Hugo Chavez); Houston's Aramco Services Company (a wholly-owned subsidiary of Saudi Arabian Oil Company, the national oil company of Saudi Arabia); and U.S. subsidiaries of the CITIC Group (the state-owned investment company of the People's Republic of China) and OAO Gazprom (the world's largest natural gas company, controlled by the Russian government).[48]

These foreign-controlled domestic companies have a demonstrated desire and capacity to influence Federal elections and elected officials. Contributions by political action committees (PACs) of foreign-parent companies have risen every election cycle in the last decade, more than doubling from roughly $7.7 million in 2000 to roughly $16.9 million in 2008.[49] Records of lobbying disclosures by such companies pursuant to the Foreign Agents Registration Act reveal extensive, well-funded attempts to influence elected officials.[50] One specific example is particularly illustrative: The U.S. subsidiary of a foreign-controlled energy company has spent over $20 million on lobbying activity since January 2009, increased its contributing activity through its PAC, made independent expenditures to defeat a state ballot initiative, and made corporate donations to Republican and Democratic governors' associations even after pledging to its shareholders that it would not make political expenditures.[51]

And now after Citizens United, these foreign-parent U.S. companies would be free to use their general treasuries for political spending--general treasuries that had total receipts in 2005 of approximately $3.5 trillion.[52]

H.R. 5175 strengthens current law by closing this Citizens United loophole to ensure that foreign corporations--and foreign governments--are not permitted to spend unlimited sums through their United States subsidiaries or affiliates in an effort to influence American elections. H.R. 5175 does this by defining ``foreign nationals'' as any corporation where foreign nationals have the ability to direct, dictate or control the decision making process as it pertains to interests in the U.S.

H.R. 5175 also extends the existing prohibition on contributions and expenditures by foreign nationals to include domestic corporations by banning campaign expenditures from: a corporation whose voting shares are 20 percent or more owned by a foreign principal;[53] corporations where a majority of the board of directors are foreign nationals; and corporations in which a foreign national or nationals have the power to direct, dictate or control the decision making with respect to the corporation's interests in the United States. H.R. 5175 clarifies that foreign persons are not permitted to use U.S. corporations to engage in activities that are and should be limited to U.S. citizens. In doing so, this bill simply reinforces what Congress has already done in numerous other areas of law, including purchases of stock of

U.S. companies involved in telecommunications, airlines, defense contracting, maritime shipping, fishing, banking, mutual funds, nuclear energy, or any activity foreign control of which is deemed a threat to national security.[54]

The threat of foreign government involvement in U.S. elections is real, and preventing the threat of foreign influence in U.S. elections is necessary to protect our democracy. In order to ensure compliance with the new rules of H.R. 5175, CEOs of a corporation are required to file an annual certification with the FEC prior to the corporation making any contribution or expenditure in that year with regard to a U.S. election, attesting that the company is not prohibited from making the contribution or expenditure by the new foreign national rules. H.R. 5175 serves a vital governmental interest by preventing the reality or appearance of foreign intervention in U.S. elections.

H.R. 5175 Treats All Organizations Equally

The DISCLOSE Act is fair and equitable, and not partisan, in its impact. It applies alike to corporations, labor unions, trade associations and non-profit advocacy organizations and does not play political favorites.

H.R. 5175 provides prompt and honest disclosure of political spending by all those seeking to influence our elections. The vast majority of the bill deals with disclosure, and everyone has to disclose. Both unions and corporations are required to make full disclosure, and to stand by their advertisements. Both are required to have their lobbyists disclose their expenditures. The bill treats similarly-situated unions and corporations exactly the same across-the-board.

The other provisions of the bill treat similarly-situated entities alike. For example, under the new contractor rules, if a union contracts with the government, it is covered by the exact same rules that cover corporations. Of course, unions do not receive TARP funds, but that should not be an argument to exempt TARP recipients. H.R. 5175's foreign corporation rules are principally focused on foreign investors and foreign sovereign wealth funds that dominate and control U.S. subsidiaries.

H.R. 5175 Strengthens Rules on Coordination

The Citizens United decision also allows corporations and labor unions to make campaign-related expenditures, as long as that spending is independent from any candidate or party. Campaign expenditures by corporations and unions that are coordinated with a candidate or party are still restricted. Thus, the definition of ``coordination" becomes the important line between spending by a corporation or union which is permissible, and that which is not.[55]

H.R. 5175 strengthens and codifies existing FEC regulations that define the types of public communications that are subject to the coordination standard. The bill prevents organizations from coordinating their campaign-related expenditures with candidates and parties in violation of rules that require these expenditures to be independent. Current FEC rules bar outside spenders from coordinating with congressional candidates and parties about ads that refer to the candidate and are distributed within 90 days of a primary election or within 90 days of the general election. For Presidential contests, current FEC rules prohibit coordination on ads that reference a presidential candidate in the period beginning 120 days before a state's Presidential primary election and continuing in that state through the general election.

For House and Senate races, the legislation would ban coordination between an outside spender and the candidate on ads referencing a Congressional candidate in the time period starting 90 days before the primary and continuing through the general election. For presidential races, the legislation would ban such coordination during the period from 120 days before the first presidential primary through the general election. For the period outside the window, existing law remains in effect.

Additionally, H.R. 5175 provides that any payment by a political party committee for the direct costs of an ad or other communication made on behalf of a candidate affiliated with the party is treated as a contribution to the candidate only if the communication is directed or controlled by the candidate. Party-paid communications that are not directed or controlled by the candidate are not subject to limits on the party's contributions or expenditures.

H.R. 5175 Improves Disclosure by Lobbying Organizations

The DISCLOSE Act incorporates new reporting requirements on independent expenditures and electioneering communications for registered lobbyists, which will improve the transparency of lobbying activities. All registrants under the Lobbying Disclosure Act must disclose the date and amount of each independent expenditure or electioneering communication greater than $1,000 and the name of each candidate referred to or supported or opposed following information on their periodic lobbying disclosure reports.

This provision will improve disclosure of activities by lobbyists, who are in the business of trying to influence government decisions. When lobbyists or lobbying organizations make campaign expenditures to influence elections, they are often done as a part of their efforts to influence legislation.[56] Requiring campaign spending by registered lobbyists to be reported together with their other lobbying activities will give the public better access to the full picture of how lobbyists operate to affect government outcomes.

The comprehensive disclosure provisions of H.R. 5175 will provide the public with a check on the ability of lobbyists to exert undue influence over elected officials.

Improvements Made to H.R. 5175 During Committee Mark-up

A number of amendments to the DISCLOSE Act were adopted during committee mark-up that reflects the debate within the Committee and an effort to adopt measures where a bipartisan consensus could be found. The adopted amendments strengthen the following sections:

Ban on Contributions and Expenditures by Foreign Nationals

A new section was added to permit U.S. citizens employed by U.S. subsidiaries of foreign countries to form and make voluntary contributions to separate segregated funds, or political action committees (PACs), provided that the PACs do not accept any contributions from foreign nationals, and no foreign national has the ``power to direct, dictate or control the establishment or administration of the fund." This amendment protects a U.S. citizen's First Amendment rights, codifies existing FEC regulations, and reasonably ensures that foreign nationals cannot use U.S. subsidiaries as a vehicle to influence American elections.

An amendment was also adopted that provides charitable and civic donations and PAC contributions and expenditures may be made without a prior certification regarding foreign national status. The Committee believes that certification regarding these payments is unnecessary.

Coordinated Communications

Technical amendments have been made to clarify the purpose of this section and conform the definition of ``public communication" to that contained in the regulations of the Federal Election Commission. The amendment exempts from the definition of ``coordination" any information a ``person" provides to a candidate or committee regarding that person's position on a legislative or policy matter, so long as that person and the candidate or committee do not discuss a campaign for Federal office. Current FEC regulations on coordination which allow for ``safe harbors" and ``firewalls" were also preserved.

Electioneering Communication

The amendment requires all filing of independent expenditure and electioneering communication reports to be done electronically. The FEC is also required to ensure that independent expenditure reports are publicly available through the Commission website within 24 hours after receipt in a manner that is downloadable in bulk and machine readable.

Another amendment was adopted that requires any independent expenditures or electioneering communications valued over $10,000 to be filed electronically in a manner that is searchable, sortable, and downloadable. This type of filing discloses information to voters more quickly, and cuts down on unnecessary data entry by the FEC, making it faster for covered organizations to comply with disclosure requirements on their own Web sites.

Additional Information to Be Included in Reports on Disbursements by Covered Organizations

These amendments close a loophole that exempts the reporting of transfers that are commercial transactions occurring in the ordinary course of business, clarifies the rules regarding the deeming of transfers by a person or a covered organization made for the purpose of making public expenditures so that they are clearer in capturing actual examples of solicitation, and exempts from reporting internal transfers made within covered organizations such as dues between state and local and national organizations or membership dues between national branches of membership organizations and their state affiliates, like the Sierra Club or NRA.

CEO Certification

Written certification notice deadlines requiring a CEO to provide written confirmation after a donor and a covered organization have mutually agreed that a donation or transfer is not to be used for political activity were extended from seven to thirty days. The revisions also allow a CEO to appoint an appropriate designee to handle the certification and modify the requirements of the certification.

Disclaimer Statements on Certain Communications

A ``hardship'' exemption was added to the mandatory radio and television disclaimers if the communication is of such ``short duration'' that the disclaimer statement constitutes a ``disproportionate amount of the communication's content,'' as determined by regulations to be promulgated by the FEC. This provision addresses the criticism that the disclaimer requirements in the bill as introduced were too onerous and would dilute the ability of speakers to deliver their political message in short ads, and unfairly increase the cost and burden of political ads.

A new provision was added to the DISCLOSE Act to require spoken disclosure of the top two funders during a radio ad, increasing accountability of radio ads.

Disclosures by Covered Organizations of Information on Campaign Related Activity

The bill was amended to require covered organizations who maintain an Internet site to post on their Internet site a hyperlink to the location on the Internet site of the FEC which contains its reports to the FEC on its public independent expenditures and electioneering communications. The covered organization will be required to post this hyperlink on their Internet site 24 hours after the FEC post such reports and for a 1-year period, which provides the public with easy access to corporate disclosure reports.

Government Contractor Threshold

The threshold on government contractors provision was raised to $7 million, reflecting the standard generally applied by the Small Business Administration to determine small business status.

Disclosure for Political Robocalls Attacking or Defending Candidates for Federal Office

The bill was amended to establish disclosure requirements for political robocalls attacking or defending candidates for Federal office. This amendment preserves the legitimate uses of political robocalls. With the addition of a disclosure statement, voters immediately know who is responsible for the call, and cannot be misled into blaming a candidate for harassing calls that the candidate did not originate.

Protecting Internet Communications

An amendment was adopted that codified current Federal Election Commission regulations to guarantee that Internet communications will not be treated as general public political advertising under the Commission's regulations, unless the communication was placed for a fee on another person's Web site. This amendment will protect free speech and the free exchange of ideas and debate over the Internet.

These amendments have improved H.R. 5175 by facilitating greater transparency and disclosure for federal elections.

Conclusion

The DISCLOSE Act is a careful and constitutional response to certain of the likely consequences of the Citizens United decision, and it serves to promote democratic deliberation through transparency and accountability in our nation's elections. H.R. 5175 is intended to provide shareholders and the public with information that the Supreme Court has recognized is essential to hold them accountable when they choose to participate in electoral activity. Voters have the right to know who is attempting to influence their vote, and enactment of the DISCLOSE Act will help to assure that right.

Committee Consideration of H.R. 5175

Introduction and Referral

On April 29, 2010, Representative Van Hollen of Maryland, Representative Brady of Pennsylvania, Representative Castle of Delaware, and Representative Jones of North Carolina, introduced H.R. 5175, which was referred to the Committee on House Administration, with an additional referral to the Committee on the Judiciary.

Hearings

On February 3, 2010, the Committee on House Administration held a hearing entitled ``Defining the Future of Campaign Finance in an Age of Supreme Court Activism.'' The following members were present at the hearing: Chairman Robert Brady, Representative Zoe Lofgren, Representative Michael Capuano, Representative Susan Davis, Representative Artur Davis, Ranking Minority Member Dan Lungren, Representative Kevin McCarthy, and Representative Gregg Harper.

Witnesses

1. Mr. Robert Lenhard--Of Counsel, Covington & Burling LLP
2. Ms. Judith A. Browne-Dianis--Co-Director, Advancement Project
3. Ms. Mary G. Wilson--President, League of Women Voters
4. Ms. Ciara Torres-Spelliscy--Counsel, Brennan Center for Justice
5. Ms. Allison Hayward--Assistant Professor of Law, George Mason University School of Law
6. Mr. Steve Simpson--Senior Attorney, Institute for Justice

On May 6, 2010, the Committee on House Administration held a hearing entitled ``H.R. 5175, the DISCLOSE ACT, Democracy is Strengthened by Casting Light on Spending in Elections." The following members were present at the hearing: Chairman Robert Brady, Representative Zoe Lofgren, Representative Michael Capuano, Representative Susan Davis, Representative Charles Gonzalez, Ranking Minority Member Dan Lungren, Representative Kevin McCarthy, and Representative Gregg Harper.

Witnesses

1. Mr. Donald J. Simon--Partner, Sonosky, Chambers, Sachse, Enderson, & Perry, LLP
2. Mr. Nick Nyhart--President & CEO, Public Campaign
3. The Honorable Theodore B. Olson--Partner, Gibson, Dunn & Crutcher, LLP
4. Mr. David Bossie--President, Citizens United
5. Ms. Lisa Gilbert--Democracy Advocate, U.S. PIRG
6. Mr. Craig Holman--Legislative Representative, Public Citizen

On May 11, 2010, the Committee on House Administration held a hearing entitled ``Additional Discussion on H.R. 5175, the DISCLOSE ACT, Democracy is Strengthened by Casting Light on Spending in Elections." The following members were present at the hearing: Chairman Robert Brady, Representative Zoe Lofgren, Representative Michael Capuano, Ranking Minority Member Dan Lungren, and Representative Gregg Harper.

Witnesses

1. The Honorable Trevor Potter--President and General Counsel, Campaign Legal Center
2. Mr. John C. Coates--Professor of Law and Economics, Harvard Law School
3. Ms. Elizabeth Lynch--Attorney, China Law & Policy
4. The Honorable Michael Toner--Partner, Bryan Cave, LLP
5. Mr. William McGinley--Attorney, Patton Boggs, LLP

Markup

On May 20, 2010, the Committee met to mark up H.R. 5175. The Committee ordered H.R. 5175 reported favorably, as amended, by a voice vote, with a quorum present. Chairman

Brady offered a ``Chairman's Mark" as an amendment in the nature of a substitute, which became the vehicle for perfecting amendments.

During the markup the following seven amendments to the Brady substitute were agreed to by a voice vote.

Rep. Davis (of California) Amendment to Brady Substitute

Representative Davis of California offered an amendment to the Brady substitute to require that any independent expenditures or electioneering communications valued over $10,000 will be filed electronically in a manner that is searchable, sortable, and downloadable, with either the Commission's downloadable, free filing software, FEC.gov's web-accessible entry form, or Commission-approved third-party software. The amendment was agreed to by a voice vote.

Rep. Mccarthy Amendment #6 to the Brady Substitute

Representative McCarthy offered an amendment to the Brady substitute to provide that charitable and civic donations and PAC contributions and expenditures may be made without a prior certification regarding foreign national status. The amendment was agreed to by a voice vote.

Rep. McCarthy Amendment #11A to Brady Substitute

Representative McCarthy offered an amendment to the Brady substitute to provide that communications disseminated over the Internet will not be treated as a form of general public political advertising subject to the Federal Election Campaign Act, provided that the communication was not placed for a fee on another person's Web site. The amendment was agreed to by a voice vote.

Rep. Lofgren Amendment #1 to Brady Substitute

Representative Lofgren offered an amendment to the Brady substitute to provide technical changes regarding the mislabeling of Subtitle A and B as well as to clarify in Section 103 that sharing information regarding legislative or policy positions does not fall under the coordination rules as long as there is no discussion between the person and the candidate regarding the candidate's campaign as opposed to any federal campaign. The amendment also corrected language in Section 102(d) of the Act. The amendment was agreed to by a voice vote.

Rep. Lofgren Amendment #2 to Brady Substitute

Representative Lofgren offered an amendment to the Brady substitute to amend Section 318 of the Federal Election Campaign Act of 1971, as amended, to require a disclaimer at the beginning of political robo-calls identifying who is funding the call. The amendment was agreed to by a voice vote.

Rep. Lofgren Amendment #3 to Brady Substitute

Representative Lofgren offered an amendment to the Brady substitute to amend Section 101(b) to raise the threshold level at which government contractors would be banned from making independent expenditures and electioneering communications to those contractors with contracts in excess of $7 million dollars. The amendment was agreed to by a voice vote.

Rep. Capuano Amendment #4 to Brady Substitute

Representative Capuano offered an amendment to the Brady substitute to require spoken disclosure of the `Top 2 Funders' during a radio advertisement. The amendment was agreed to by a voice vote.

Section-by-Section Summary Of H.R. 5175

(AS ORDERED REPORTED)

Section One--Short title

Establishes the short title of ``Democracy is Strengthened by Casting Light on Spending in Elections Act,'' or the DISCLOSE Act. This section also provides a table of contents for the bill.

Section Two--Findings

Among the principal findings were:

- Throughout the history of the United States people have been concerned about the power of special interests to control our democratic processes.
- The U.S. Supreme Court's decision in Citizens United v. F.E.C. reversed existing jurisprudence when it permitted corporations and labor unions to spend unlimited sums from their treasury accounts to influence elections.
- Congress must take action to ensure the public has all the information necessary to make informed decisions and exercise its free speech and voting rights.
- Government contracts must be awarded based on an objective evaluation of how well bidders or potential contractors meet relevant statutory criteria, and the process must avoid the appearance of, or actual, improper influence.
- Independent expenditures and electioneering communications benefiting particular candidates or disfavoring opponents can lead to apparent and actual access, influence, and or even quid pro quo arrangements, and prohibiting expenditures and communications will ensure that government officials involved in the contracting process do not influence the contract process inappropriately.
- Prohibiting independent expenditures and electioneering communications by persons negotiating for or performing government contract work will prevent such persons from feeling pressure to make political expenditures in order to maximize their chances of receiving government contracts.
- The U.S. Supreme Court's decision in Citizens United v. F.E.C. has provided the means by which U.S. corporations controlled by foreign entities can freely spend money to influence elections.
- The Federal Government has broad constitutional power to protect American interests and sovereignty from foreign interference, and Congress has a clear interest in minimizing foreign intervention as well as the perception of foreign intervention in our elections.
- It has been the consistent view of Congress and the courts that coordinated expenditures in campaigns are no different in nature from contributions, and that independent campaign expenditures have the potential to give rise to the reality of

corruption to the same degree as direct contributions to candidates, and thus have the potential to lessen the public's trust and faith in the rules and integrity of the election process.

- The government has a compelling interest in making sure that political expenditures that are defacto coordinated with a candidate are treated as such to prevent corruption and the appearance of corruption.
- The American people have a compelling interest in knowing who is funding independent expenditures and electioneering communication to influence elections, and the government has a compelling interest in providing that information to the public so that it may make informed voting decisions.
- Effective disclaimers and prompt disclosure of expenditures, and the disclosing of funding sources for those expenditures, can provide shareholders, voters, and citizens with the information to evaluate the actions of special interests.
- Transparency promotes accountability, increases the fund of information available to the public concerning support given to candidates by special interests, sheds the light of publicity on political spending, and encourages leaders of organizations to act only upon legitimate organizational purposes.
- Ensuring effective disclosure is particularly important to address the anticipated increase in special interest spending resulting from the Supreme Court's decision in Citizens United v. F.E.C.
- More rigorous disclosure and disclaimer requirements are necessary to protect against the evasion of current rules. Robust disclaimer requirements are necessary to ensure that the electorate is informed about who is paying for a particular election-related communication and shareholders are aware of their organizations' election-related spending.
- In recent years, scandals involving undue lobbyist influence over matters of public policy and legislation have lowered public trust in government.
- One way in which lobbyists may unduly influence Federal officials is through independent expenditures targeting elected officials.
- Disclosure of independent expenditures by lobbyists will allow the public to examine connections between such spending and official actions as well as limit the ability of lobbyists to exert an undue influence on elected officials.

TITLE I--REGULATION OF CERTAIN POLITICAL SPENDING

Sec. 101. Prohibiting Independent Expenditures and Electioneering Communications by Government Contractors

Prohibits a person (including a corporation) who has a contract with the United States government valued at $7,000,000 or more from making ``campaign related expenditures'' (defined as independent expenditures and electioneering communications).

This threshold reflects the standard generally applied by the Small Business Administration to determine small business status.

Prohibits a person (including a corporation) who enters into negotiations for financial assistance under TARP from making ``campaign related expenditures" until the negotiations end or the financial assistance is repaid.

Sec. 102. Application of Ban on Contributions and Expenditures by Foreign Nationals to Foreign-Controlled Domestic Corporations

Bans contributions and expenditures by any domestic corporation in which (1) a foreign national owns 20% or more of the voting shares, (2) a majority of the board of directors are foreign nationals, or (3) a foreign national has the power to direct, dictate or control the decision-making process of the corporation with respect to its interests in the U.S. or with respect to activities in connection with a federal, state, or local election.

Requires a corporation's CEO, or highest ranking official, to file an annual certification with the FEC, certifying that the corporation is not foreign-controlled, prior to making ``campaign related expenditures."

Sec. 102 does not limit the ability of any corporation--other than a foreign national--to maintain a separate segregated fund, provided that no foreign national or nationals make contributions into the fund or direct, dictate, or control the fund.

Provides that charitable and civic donations, and contributions and expenditures by a political action committee may be made without prior certification regarding foreign national status.

Sec. 103. Treatment of Payments for Coordinated Communications as Contributions

Defines a coordinated communication as (1) a ``covered communication" made in cooperation, consultation, or concert with, or at the request or suggestion of a candidate, or a political committee of a political party, or (2) any communication that republishes, disseminates, or distributes campaign material prepared by a candidate or an authorized committee of a candidate.

A ``covered communication" is defined as a ``public communication as defined in section 301(22)" that refers to a clearly defined candidate for Federal office and is distributed in the candidate's district during the applicable election period.

For Presidential candidates, a ``covered communication" is a ``public communication" that refers to the candidate during the period beginning 120 days before the first primary and ending on the day of the general election. The applicable election period for a candidate for any other Federal office is 90 days before the primary or nominating convention and ending with the date of the general election for such office.

``Covered communications" exclude both communications that qualify for the ``media exemption" and communications that constitute a candidate debate or forum (if made by the debate or forum sponsor). Coordination also may not be found based solely on sharing of information or policy positions, provided that there is no discussion regarding the candidate's campaign.

This section also clarifies that solely sharing information about a legislative or policy position does not warrant coordination as long as there is no discussion regarding any campaign for Federal office between the person and candidate or committee; and adds language to preserve current FEC regulations on coordination which allow for ``safe harbors" and ``firewalls."

Sec. 104. Treatment of Political Party Communications Made on Behalf of Candidates

Excludes political party communications from being treated as contributions to candidates as long as the communications are not controlled by or at the direction of the candidate or an authorized committee of the candidate.

TITLE II--PROMOTING EFFECTIVE DISCLOSURE OF CAMPAIGN RELATED ACTIVITY

Subtitle A--Treatment of Independent Expenditures and Electioneering Communications Made by All Persons

Sec. 201. Independent Expenditures

Revises definition of independent expenditure to include express advocacy of the election or defeat of a candidate, or its functional equivalent.

Expands reporting requirements to include a report be filed within 24 hours of any independent expenditure that is either (1) greater than or equal to $10,000 prior to twenty days before an election, or (2) greater than or equal to $1,000 within twenty days of an election.

Requires the Federal Election Commission to ensure that the independent expenditure reports be publicly available though the Commission's website not later than 24 hours after receipt in a manner that is downloadable in bulk and machine readable.

Sec. 202. Electioneering Communications

Expands the period during which communications are treated as electioneering communications to 120 days before the general election.

Requires the electronic filing of all electioneering communication reports and that the Federal Election Commission make them publicly available through its website not later than 24 hours after receipt in a manner that is downloadable in bulk and machine readable.

Subtitle B--Expanded Requirements for Corporations and Other Organizations

Sec. 211. Additional Information Required to Be Included in Reports on Disbursements by Covered Organizations

Requires corporations, labor unions, 527 Organizations, and Section 501(c)(4) and (6) organizations making independent expenditures over $10,000 in political campaigns to report: (1) all donors making designated donations or payments for campaign related activities in the aggregate amount of $600; (2) all donors making unrestricted payments in an aggregated amount greater than or equal to $600 or in an aggregate amount greater than or equal to $6,000 if the disbursements were made exclusively from the organizations Campaign Related Activity Account. In addition, all reporting must include the specific candidate the donation was made for as for as well as the specific expenditure it was designated for.

Specifies that an organization that transfers amounts to another ``person" (other than the covered organization itself) to make an independent expenditure and electioneering communication is considered to have made an independent expenditure and electioneering communication and is thus subject to the reporting requirements. The transfer of funds for commercial transactions is not subject to these reporting requirements.

Defines the following scenarios in which a person or a covered organization is deemed to have transferred funds to another person for the purpose of making independent expenditures: (1) if the person designates, requests or suggests that the amount be used for public independent expenditures and the person to whom the amounts were transferred agrees to do so or does so; (2) if the person making the public independent expenditure or another person acting on that person's behalf expressly solicited the person for a donation for any public independent expenditure; (3) the person and person to whom amounts were transferred engaged in substantial written or oral discussion regarding the making or paying for any public independent expenditure; (4) the person or the persons transferred knew or had reason to know of the covered organization's intent to make public independent expenditures; or (5) the person or the person to whom amounts were transferred made a public independent expenditure during the 2-year period which ends on the date on which the amounts were transferred.

Adds language in Section 211 to clarify that a commercial transaction occurring in the ordinary course of business between the person and the person to whom the amounts were transferred shall not be deemed an independent expenditure, unless there is affirmative evidence that the amounts were transferred for the purpose of making a public independent expenditure.

Specifies that donations designated for campaign activity related to other candidates and elections should be excluded when determining the amount of donations to report, and that any amounts paid from a separate segregated fund are also excluded in determining the amount of public independent expenditures.

Sec. 212. Rules Regarding Use of General Treasury Funds by Covered Organizations for Campaign-Related Activity

Permits all covered organizations to make disbursements for campaign-related activity using: amounts paid or donated to the organization that have been designated by the donor for such purposes; unrestricted donor payments made to the organization; and/or other funds of the organization such as funds received from commercial activities.

Provides that if a covered organization and a person mutually agree that the person's donation, payment or transfer is not to be used for campaign-related activity, the organization will transmit to that person within 30 days a written certification by the chief financial officer or the highest ranking financial official of the organization that the person's donation, payment or transfer will not be used for campaign-related activity.

Requires that the CEO or highest ranking official or designee of an covered organization making disbursements for campaign related activity file a statement with the Federal Election Commission not later than 15 days after the end of the quarter certifying the following: (1) the campaign related activity was not in any way coordinated with any candidate or agent or authorized committee of such candidate, (2) the CEO or highest ranking official of the organization has reviewed and approved each statement, (3) the statement is complete and accurate, (4) the expenditure is in compliance with this Act, and (5) there are no funds used that were designated by a donor to specifically not be used for campaign-related activities.

Sec. 213. Optional Use of Separate Account by Covered Organizations for Campaign-Related Activity

Provides that all covered organizations may establish a Campaign-Related Activity Account to make disbursements for campaign-related activity.

Prohibits covered organizations setting up Campaign-Related Activity Accounts from making disbursements for campaign-related activity from any other account.

Requires Campaign-Related Activity Accounts to be used exclusively for campaign-related activity.

Restricts deposits into the Campaign-Related Activity Accounts to the following: those donated for campaign-related activity; those that are not designated for a specific candidate or election; those that are in response to a solicitation for funds; and/or those that are from the organizations' general treasury funds.

Specifies that the establishment of Campaign-Related Activity Accounts shall not be treated as political committee.

Requires covered organizations to reduce the amount of its revenues available for deposit into the Campaign-Related Activity Account by the donation made during the year when a donor notifies the organization in writing that its payment may not be used for campaign-related activities.

Sec. 214. Modification of Rules Relating to Disclaimer Statements Required for Certain Communications

Requires corporations, labor unions, 527 organizations, and Section 501(c)(4) and (6) organizations to issue individual disclosure statements or organizational disclosure statements on all radio and television ads. The provision provides a specific script for the individual and organization disclosure statements and requires them to be transmitted through audio for radio ads and clearly displayed in print for six seconds on television ads.

Requires all electioneering communication or public communication expenditures paid for in whole or in part by a covered organization/person to include a Significant Funder Disclosure statement. The provision provides a specific script for the individual and organization Significant Funder Disclosure statements and requires them to be transmitted through audio for radio ads and clearly displayed in print for six seconds on television ads.

Requires television advertising produced by covered organizations to include a full screen disclosure of its Top Five Funders (the largest payments of any type), and their donations amounts. Radio advertising will require spoken disclosure of top 2 funders of the advertising. Also provides for a hardship exemption to mandatory radio and television disclaimers if the communication is so short that the disclaimer statement constitutes a ``disproportionate amount of the communication's content"

Defines Significant Funder for independent expenditures and electioneering communications as: (1) person making payment greater or equal to $100,000 and who has designated such funds for that specific independent expenditure/electioneering communication, (2) person making payment greater or equal to $100,000 and who has designated such funds for the same election or in support of the same candidate, (3) person making the largest payment for independent expenditure/electioneering communication in response to a solicitation of funds to be sued for campaign-related activity, and (4) person who made the largest unrestricted donor payment.

Requires a disclaimer at the beginning of political robo-calls identifying who is the funder of the robo-call.

Subtitle C--Reporting Requirements for Registered Lobbyists

Sec. 221. Requiring Registered Lobbyists to Report Information on Independent Expenditures and Electioneering Communications

Requires registered lobbyists to report the amount of independent expenditures and electioneering communications greater than or equal to $1,000 along with the name of each candidate being supported or opposed and the amount spent supporting or opposing each such candidate.

TITLE III--DISCLOSURE BY COVERED ORGANIZATIONS OF INFORMATION ON CAMPAIGN-RELATED ACTIVITY

Sec. 301. Requiring Disclosure by Covered Organizations of Information on Campaign-Related Activity

Requires corporations, labor unions, 527 organizations, and Section 501(c)(4) and (6) organizations that submit regular, periodic reports to its shareholders, members or donors to include in each report the date of the independent expenditure or electioneering communication, the amount, the name of the candidate identified, the office sought by the candidate, whether the independent expenditure or electioneering communication was in support or opposition, the name of the recipient of transferred funds (if applicable), the source of the funds, and other information that may be required by the Federal Election Commission.

Requires any covered organization which maintains a website to post a link on their website to their reports on public independent expenditures and electioneering communications to the Federal Election Commission 24 hours after the Commission makes such reports publicly available and for that the link remain on the site for a 1-year period.

TITLE IV-- OTHER PROVISIONS

Sec. 401. Judicial review

Requires any action for declaratory or injunctive relief challenging provisions within this Act on constitutional grounds to first be filed in the United States District Court for the District of Columbia and on appeal to the Court of Appeals for the District of Columbia Circuit. In addition this provision requires any compliant to be delivered to the Clerk of the House and the Secretary of the Senate, as directs that the courts expedite to the greatest extent possible the disposition of any action and appeal.

Provides any Congressional Member with the ability to intervene in any action related to the constitutionality of this Act, and the ability to bring an action, subject to the judicial review established in the Act, for injunctive relief to challenge the constitutionality of any provision within the legislation.

Specifies that if any provision in this Act is ruled unconstitutional the remainder of the Act shall not be affected by the holding.

Establishes an effective date for all provisions of 30 days after enactment of the legislation.

Matters Required Under the Rules of the House

COMMITTEE ROLL CALL VOTES

Clause 3(b) of House rule XIII requires the results of each recorded vote on an amendment or motion to report, together with the names of those voting for and against, to be printed in the committee report. Chairman Brady introduced an amendment in the nature of a substitute to address issues that were raised during the course of the Committee hearings and meetings with various stakeholders.

Rep. Lungren Amendment #2 to Brady Substitute

Representative Lungren offered an amendment to the Brady substitute to provide that the prohibition on expenditures by government contractors shall also apply to labor unions having representational contracts with the government. The amendment was not agreed to by a record vote of 3 ayes to 5 noes.

Member	Ayes	Noes	Present
Rep. Lofgren	--	X	--
Rep. Capuano	--	X	--
Rep. Gonzalez	--	--	--
Rep. Davis (CA)	--	X	--
Rep. Davis (AL)	--	X	--
Rep. Lungren	X	--	--
Rep. McCarthy	X	--	--
Rep. Harper	X	--	--
Rep. Brady	--	X	--
Total	3	5	--

Rep. Lungren Amendment #5 to Brady Substitute

Representative Lungren offered an amendment to the Brady substitute to require that the highest ranking official of a labor organization certify that no dues were received from any foreign national prior to the making of an independent expenditure or electioneering communication. The amendment was not agreed to by a record vote of 3 ayes to 6 noes.

Member	Ayes	Noes	Present
Rep. Lofgren	--	X	--
Rep. Capuano	--	X	--
Rep. Gonzalez	--	X	--
Rep. Davis (CA)	--	X	--
Rep. Davis (AL)	--	X	--
Rep. Lungren	X	--	--
Rep. McCarthy	X	--	--
Rep. Harper	X	--	--
Rep. Brady	--	X	--
Total	3	6	--

Rep. Harper Amendment #10 to Brady Substitute

Representative Harper offered an amendment to the Brady substitute to delay the Act's effective date to January 1, 2011. The amendment was not agreed to by a record vote of 3 ayes to 5 noes.

Member	Ayes	Noes	Present
Rep. Lofgren	--	X	--
Rep. Capuano	--	X	--
Rep. Gonzalez	--	X	--
Rep. Davis (CA)	--	X	--
Rep. Davis (AL)	--	--	--
Rep. Lungren	X	--	--
Rep. McCarthy	X	--	--
Rep. Harper	X	--	--
Rep. Brady	--	X	--
Total	3	5	--

Rep. Mccarthy Amendment #7 to Brady Substitute

Representative McCarthy offered an amendment to the Brady substitute to provide that no funds obtained by a union through a government-administered payroll deduction program may be used for political expenditures. The amendment was not agreed to by a record vote of 3 ayes to 5 noes.

Member	Ayes	Noes	Present
Rep. Lofgren	--	--	--
Rep. Capuano	--	--	--
Rep. Gonzalez	--	--	--
Rep. Davis (CA)	--	--	--
Rep. Davis (AL)	--		--
Rep. Lungren	X	X	--
Rep. McCarthy	X	X	--
Rep. Harper	X	X	--
Rep. Brady	--	X	--
Total	3	5	--

Rep. McCarthy amendment #9 to Brady substitute

Representative McCarthy offered an amendment to the Brady substitute to lower the contribution amount at which donor disclosure is required to the same as the itemized level for political committees. The amendment was not agreed to by a record vote of 3 ayes to 4 noes.

Member	Ayes	Noes	Present
Rep. Lofgren	--	X	--
Rep. Capuano	--	X	--
Rep. Gonzalez	--	--	--
Rep. Davis (CA)	--	X	--
Rep. Davis (AL)	--	--	--
Rep. Lungren	X	--	--
Rep. McCarthy	X	--	--
Rep. Harper	X	--	--
Rep. Brady	--	X	--
Total	3	4	--

Rep. Lungren amendment #13 to Brady substitute

Representative Lungren offered an amendment to the Brady substitute to ban all political expenditures by labor organizations representing employees of government contractors.

The amendment was not agreed to by a record vote of 3 ayes to 4 noes.

Member	Ayes	Noes	Present
Rep. Lofgren	--	X	--
Rep. Capuano	--	X	--
Rep. Gonzalez	--	--	--
Rep. Davis (CA)	--	X	--
Rep. Davis (AL)	--	--	--
Rep. Lungren	X	--	--
Rep. McCarthy	X	--	--
Rep. Harper	X	--	--
Rep. Brady	--	X	--
Total	3	4	--

Following consideration of perfecting amendments, the Committee agreed to the Brady amendment in the nature of a substitute, as amended, by a record vote of 5 ayes to 3 noes.

Member	Ayes	Noes	Present
Rep. Lofgren	X	--	--
Rep. Capuano	X	--	--
Rep. Gonzalez	--	--	--
Rep. Davis (CA)	X	--	--
Rep. Davis (AL)	X	--	--
Rep. Lungren	--	X	--
Rep. McCarthy	--	X	--
Rep. Harper	--	X	--
Rep. Brady	X	--	--
Total	5	3	--

Constitutional Authority

Clause 3(d)(1) of House rule XIII requires each committee report on a public bill or joint resolution to include a statement citing the specific constitutional power(s) granted to the Congress on which the Committee relies for enactment of the measure under consideration. The Committee states that Article 1, Section 4 of the U.S. Constitution grants Congress the authority to make laws governing the time, place and manner of holding Federal elections.

Congressional Budget Office Estimate

Clause 3(c)(3) of House rule XIII requires the report of a committee on a measure which has been approved by the committee to include a cost estimate prepared by the Director of the Congressional Budget Office pursuant to section 402 of the CBA, if timely submitted. The Director submitted the following estimate:

May 24, 2010.
Hon. Robert A. Brady,

Chairman, Committee on House Administration,
House of Representatives, Washington, DC.

Dear Mr. Chairman: The Congressional Budget Office has prepared the enclosed cost estimate for H.R. 5175, the DISCLOSE Act.

If you wish further details on this estimate, we will be pleased to provide them. The CBO staff contact is Matthew Pickford.

Sincerely,
Douglas W. Elmendorf.
Enclosure.

H.R. 5175--Disclose Act

Summary: H.R. 5175 would amend the Federal Election Campaign Act of 1971 to require that additional campaign-spending information be reported to the Federal Election Commission (FEC) and that additional information be made available to the public. In addition, the legislation would extend or create new prohibitions on political spending by certain government contractors, recipients of funds from the Troubled Asset Relief Program (TARP), and companies controlled by foreign nationals.

CBO estimates that implementing H.R. 5175 would cost $2 million in fiscal year 2011 and about $10 million over the 2011-2015 period, subject to appropriation of the necessary funds. Those amounts would cover additional administrative costs for the FEC to ensure compliance with the bill. Enacting H.R. 5175 could increase revenues and direct spending from the collection of civil and criminal penalties; therefore, pay-as-you-go procedures would apply. However, CBO estimates that the net budgetary effect of any additional penalty collections would be negligible for each year.

H.R. 5175 contains no intergovernmental mandates as defined in the Unfunded Mandates Reform Act (UMRA) and would not affect the budgets of state, local, or tribal governments.

H.R. 5175 contains private-sector mandates, as defined in UMRA, on lobbyists, political organizations, and other entities or individuals that make political expenditures. Based on information from the FEC, CBO estimates that the aggregate cost to comply with the mandates would fall below the annual threshold established in UMRA for private-sector mandates ($141 million in 2010, adjusted annually for inflation).

Estimated cost to the Federal Government: The estimated budgetary impact of H.R. 5175 is shown in the following table.

The costs of this legislation fall within budget function 800 (general government).

2011	2012	2013	2014	2015	2011-2015
CHANGES IN SPENDING SUBJECT TO APPROPRIATION					
Estimated Authorization Level					
3	2	2	2	2	11
Estimated Outlays					
2	2	2	2	2	10

Basis of estimate: For this estimate, CBO assumes that H.R. 5175 will be enacted near the end of fiscal year 2010, that the necessary funds will be provided for each year, and that spending will follow the historical spending patterns of the FEC.

SPENDING SUBJECT TO APPROPRIATION

Based on information from the FEC, CBO estimates that the agency would spend about $1 million over the 2010-2011 period to reconfigure its information systems, write new and revise old regulations, and provide training and outreach to interested groups.

In addition, the FEC would need to ensure compliance with the bill's provisions, analyze the new reports submitted by campaigns, and investigate possible violations and complaints.

Based on information from the FEC, CBO estimates that conducting those activities would cost about $2 million a year.

Pay-as-you-go considerations: The Statutory Pay-As-You-Go Act of 2010 establishes budget reporting and enforcement procedures for legislation affecting direct spending or revenues. Enacting H.R. 5175 could increase civil and criminal fines collected for violations of the bill's provisions. Civil fines are recorded as revenues. Criminal fines are recorded as revenues, deposited in the Crime Victims Fund, and subsequently spent without further appropriation. CBO estimates that any additional collections would not be significant because of the relatively small number of cases likely to result. The net changes to outlays and revenues that are subject to pay-as-you-go procedures are shown in the following table.

Cbo Estimate of Pay-as-You-Go Effects for H.R. 5175, the Disclose Act, as Ordered Reported by the House Committee on House Administration on May 20, 2010

By fiscal year, in millions of dollars												
2010	2011	2012	2013	2014	2015	2016	2017	2018	2019	2020	2010-2015	2010-2020
NET INCREASE OR DECREASE (-) IN THE DEFICIT Statutory Pay-As-You-Go Impact												
0	0	0	0	0	0	0	0	0	0	0	0	0

Estimated impact on State, local, and tribal governments:

H.R. 5175 contains no intergovernmental mandates as defined in UMRA and would not affect the budgets of state, local, or tribal governments.

Estimated impact on the private sector: H.R. 5175 contains private-sector mandates, as defined in UMRA. Those mandates would expand reporting requirements for lobbyists, political organizations and other entities or individuals that make certain political expenditures, require new disclosures in political ads, mass mailings, and automated political calls, and expand the ban on contributions and other political expenditures by foreign nationals. Based on information from the FEC, CBO estimates that the aggregate cost to comply with the mandates would fall below the annual threshold established in UMRA for private-sector mandates ($141 million in 2010, adjusted annually for inflation).

Estimate prepared by: Federal Costs: Matthew Pickford;

Impact on State, Local, and Tribal Governments: Elizabeth Cove Delisle; Impact on the Private Sector: Paige Piper/Bach.

Estimate approved by: Theresa Gullo, Deputy Assistant Director for Budget Analysis.

Federal Mandates

Section 423 of the CBA requires a committee report on any public bill or joint resolution that includes a federal mandate to include specific information about such mandates. The Committee adopts as its own the estimate of Federal mandates prepared by the Director of the Congressional Budget Office pursuant to Section 423 of the Unfunded Mandates Reform Act (P.L. 104-4).

Preemption Clarification

Section 423 of the CBA requires a committee report on any public bill or joint resolution to include a committee statement on the extent to which the measure is intended to preempt state or local law. The Committee states that H.R. 5175 is not intended to preempt any state or local law.

Oversight Findings

Clause 3(c)(1) of rule XIII requires each committee report to contain oversight findings and recommendations required pursuant to clause 2(b)(1) of House rule X. Oversight findings are addressed elsewhere in the descriptive portions of the report. The Committee has general oversight responsibility for the Federal Election Commission.

Statement of General Peformance Goals and Objectives

Clause 3(c)(4) of House rule XIII requires committee reports to include a statement of general performance goals and objectives. H.R. 5175 will improve the transparency and integrity of the election process by increasing the disclosure of political spending in elections.

Congressional Earmarks

Clause 9 of House rule XXI requires committee reports on public bills and resolutions to contain an identification of congressional ``earmarks,'' limited tax benefits, limited tariff benefits, and the names of requesting Members. The bill as reported contains no such items.

Changes in Existing Law Made by the Bill, as Reported

In compliance with clause 3(e) of rule XIII of the Rules of the House of Representatives, changes in existing law made by the bill, as reported, are shown as follows (existing law proposed to be omitted is enclosed in black brackets, new matter is printed in italic, existing law in which no change is proposed is shown in roman):

FEDERAL ELECTION CAMPAIGN ACT OF 1971

* * * * * * *

TITLE III--DISCLOSURE OF FEDERAL CAMPAIGN FUNDS

DEFINITIONS

Sec. 301. When used in this Act:
(1) * * *

* * * * * * *

(8)(A) The term ``contribution'' includes--

(i) any gift, subscription, loan, advance, or deposit of money or anything of value made by any person for the purpose of influencing any election for Federal office; [or]

(ii) the payment by any person of compensation for the personal services of another person which are rendered to a political committee without charge for any purpose[.];

(iii) any payment made by any person (other than a candidate, an authorized committee of a candidate, or a political committee of a political party) for a coordinated communication (as determined under section 324); or

(iv) any payment by a political committee of a political party for the direct costs of a public communication (as defined in paragraph (22)) made on behalf of a candidate for Federal office who is affiliated with such party, but only if the communication is controlled by, or made at the direction of, the candidate or an authorized committee of the candidate.

* * * * * * *

(17) Independent expenditure.--The term ``independent expenditure'' means an expenditure by a person--

[(A) expressly advocating the election or defeat of a clearly identified candidate; and]

(A) that, when taken as a whole, expressly advocates the election or defeat of a clearly identified candidate, or is the functional equivalent of express advocacy because it can be interpreted by a reasonable person only as advocating the election or defeat of a candidate, taking into account whether the communication involved mentions a candidacy, a political party, or a challenger to a candidate, or takes a position on a candidate's character, qualifications, or fitness for office; and

* * * * * * *

(22) Public communication.--The term ``public communication'' means a communication by means of any broadcast, cable, or satellite communication, newspaper, magazine, outdoor advertising facility, mass mailing, or telephone bank to the general public, or any other form of general public political advertising.

A communication which is disseminated through the Internet shall not be treated as a form of general public political advertising under this paragraph unless the communication was placed for a fee on another person's Web site.

* * * * * * *

REPORTS

Sec. 304. (a) * * *

* * * * * * *

(d)(1) Any person who is required to file a statement under subsection (c) [or (g)] of this section, except statements required to be filed electronically pursuant to subsection (a)(11)(A)(i) may file the statement by facsimile device or electronic mail, in accordance with such regulations as the Commission may promulgate. Notwithstanding any other provision of this section, any person who is required to file a statement under subsection (f) or subsection (g) shall file the statement in electronic form accessible by computers, in a manner which ensures that the information provided is searchable, sortable, and downloadable.

* * * * * * *

(f) Disclosure of Electioneering Communications.--

(1) Statement required.--Every person who makes a disbursement for the direct costs of producing and airing electioneering communications in an aggregate amount in excess of $10,000 during any calendar year shall, within 24 hours of each disclosure date, [file with] electronically file with the Commission a statement containing the information described in paragraph (2). Notwithstanding any other provision of this section, the Commission shall ensure that the information required to be disclosed under this subsection is publicly available through the Commission website not later than 24 hours after receipt in a manner that is downloadable in bulk and machine readable.

(2) Contents of statement.--Each statement required to be filed under this subsection shall be made under penalty of perjury and shall contain the following information:

(A) * * *

* * * * * * *

(E) If the disbursements were paid out of a segregated bank account which consists of funds contributed solely by individuals who are United States citizens or nationals or lawfully admitted for permanent residence (as defined in section 101(a)(20) of the Immigration and Nationality Act (8 U.S.C. 1101(a)(20))) directly to this account for electioneering communications, the names and addresses of all contributors who contributed an aggregate amount of $1,000 or more to that account during the period beginning on the first day of the preceding calendar year and ending on the disclosure date. Nothing in this subparagraph is to be construed as a prohibition on the use of funds in such a segregated account for a purpose other than electioneering communications.

(F) If the disbursements were paid out of funds not described in subparagraph (E), the names and addresses of all contributors who contributed an aggregate amount of $1,000 or more to the person making the disbursement during the period beginning on the first day of the preceding calendar year and ending on the disclosure date.

* * * * * * *

(3) Electioneering communication.--For purposes of this subsection--

(A) In general.--(i) The term

``electioneering communication'' means any broadcast, cable, or satellite communication which--

(I) * * *

(II) is made within--

(aa) [60 days] 120 days before a general, special, or runoff election for the office sought by the candidate; or

* * * * * * *

(6) Disclosure of additional information by covered organizations.--

(A) Additional information.--If a covered organization files a statement under this subsection, the statement shall include, in addition to the information required under paragraph (2), the following information:

(i) If any person made a donation or payment to the covered organization during the covered organization reporting period which was provided for the purpose of being used for campaign- related activity or in response to a solicitation for funds to be used for campaign-related activity--

(I) subject to subparagraph (C), the identification of each person who made such donations or payments in an aggregate amount equal to or exceeding $1,000 during such period, presented in the order of the aggregate amount of donations or payments made by such persons during such period (with the identification of the person making the largest donation or payment appearing first); and

(II) if any person identified under subclause (I) designated that the donation or payment be used for campaign-related activity with respect to a specific election or in support of a specific candidate, the name of the election or candidate involved, and if any such person designated that the donation or payment be used for a specific electioneering communication, a description of the communication.

(ii) The identification of each person who made unrestricted donor payments to the organization during the covered organization reporting period--

(I) in an aggregate amount equal to or exceeding $1,000 during such period, if any of the disbursements made by the organization for any of the electioneering communications which are covered by the statement were not made from the organization's Campaign- Related Activity Account under section 326; or

(II) in an aggregate amount equal to or exceeding $10,000 during such period, if the disbursements made by the organization for all of the electioneering communications which are covered by the statement were made exclusively from the organization's Campaign-Related Activity Account under section 326 (but only if the organization has made deposits described in subparagraph (D) of section 326(a)(2) into that Account during such period in an aggregate amount equal to or greater than $10,000), presented in the order of the aggregate amount of payments made by such persons during such period (with the identification of the person making the largest payment appearing first).

(B) Treatment of transfers made to other persons.--

(i) In general.--For purposes of the requirement to file statements under this subsection (including the requirement under subparagraph (A) to include additional information in such statements), a covered organization which transfers amounts to another person (other than the covered organization itself) for the purpose of making an electioneering communication by that person or by any other person, or (in accordance with clause (ii)) which is deemed to have transferred amounts to another person (other than the covered organization itself) for the purpose of making an electioneering communication by that person or by any other person, shall be considered to have made a disbursement for an electioneering communication.

(ii) Rules for deeming transfers made for purpose of making communications.--

For purposes of clause (i), in determining whether a covered organization or any other person who transfers amounts to another person shall be deemed to have transferred the amounts for the purpose of making an electioneering communication, the following rules apply:

(I) The person shall be deemed to have transferred the amounts for the purpose of making an electioneering communication if--

(aa) the person designates, requests, or suggests that the amounts be used for electioneering communications and the person to whom the amounts were transferred agrees to do so or does so;

(bb) the person making the electioneering communication or another person acting on that person's behalf expressly solicited the person for a donation or payment for making or paying for any electioneering communications;

(cc) the person and the person to whom the amounts were transferred engaged in substantial written or oral discussion regarding the person either making, or donating or paying for, any electioneering communications;

(dd) the person or the person to whom the amounts were transferred knew or had reason to know of the covered organization's intent to make electioneering communications; or

(ee) the person or the person to whom the amounts were transferred made an electioneering communication during the 2-year period which ends on the date on which the amounts were transferred.

(II) The person shall not be considered to have transferred the amounts for the purpose of making an electioneering communication if the transfer was a commercial transaction occurring in the ordinary course of business between the person and the person to whom the amounts were transferred, unless there is affirmative evidence that the amounts were transferred for the purpose of making an electioneering communication.

(C) Exclusion of amounts designated for other campaign-related activity. --For purposes of subparagraph (A)(i), in determining the amount of a donation or payment made by a person which was provided for the purpose of being used for campaign-related activity or in response to a solicitation for funds to be used for campaign- related activity, there shall be excluded any amount which was designated by the person to be used--

(i) for campaign-related activity described in clause (ii) of section 325(d)(2)(A) (relating to electioneering communications) with respect to a different election, or with respect to a candidate in a different election, than an election which is the subject of any of the electioneering communications covered by the statement involved; or

(ii) for any campaign-related activity described in clause (i) of section 325(d)(2)(A) (relating to independent expenditures consisting of a public communication).

(D) Covered organization reporting period described.--In this paragraph, the ``covered organization reporting period'' is, with respect to a statement filed by a covered organization under this subsection--

(i) in the case of the first statement filed by a covered organization under this subsection which includes information required under this paragraph, the shorter of-- (I) the period which begins on the effective date of the Democracy is Strengthened by Casting Light on Spending in Elections Act and ends on the disclosure date for the statement, or

(II) the 12-month period ending on the disclosure date for the statement; and

(ii) in the case of any subsequent statement filed by a covered organization under this subsection which includes information required under this paragraph, the period occurring since the most recent statement filed by the organization which includes such information.

(E) Covered organization defined.--In this paragraph, the term ``covered organization'' means any of the following:

(i) Any corporation which is subject to section 316(a).

(ii) Any labor organization (as defined in section 316).

(iii) Any organization described in paragraph (4), (5), or (6) of section 501(c) of the Internal Revenue Code of 1986 and exempt from tax under section 501(a) of such Code.

(iv) Any political organization under section 527 of the Internal Revenue Code of 1986, other than a political committee under this Act.

(F) Other definitions.--In this paragraph, the terms ``campaign-related activity'' and ``unrestricted donor payment'' have the meaning given such terms in section 325.

[(6)] (7) Coordination with other requirements.--Any requirement to report under this subsection shall be in addition to any other reporting requirement under this Act.

[(7)] (8) Coordination with internal revenue code.--

Nothing in this subsection may be construed to establish, modify, or otherwise affect the definition of political activities or electioneering activities (including the definition of participating in, intervening in, or influencing or attempting to influence a political campaign on behalf of or in opposition to any candidate for public office) for purposes of the Internal Revenue Code of 1986.

(g) Time for Reporting Certain Expenditures.-- [(1) Expenditures aggregating $1,000.-- [(A) Initial report.--A person (including a political committee) that makes or contracts to make independent expenditures aggregating $1,000 or more after the 20th day, but more than 24 hours, before the date of an election shall file a report describing the expenditures within 24 hours.

[(B) Additional reports.--After a person files a report under subparagraph (A), the person shall file an additional report within 24 hours after each time the person makes or contracts to make independent expenditures aggregating an additional $1,000 with respect to the same election as that to which the initial report relates.

[(2) Expenditures aggregating $10,000.-- [(A) Initial report.--A person (including a political committee) that makes or contracts to make independent expenditures aggregating $10,000 or more at any time up to and including the 20th day before the date of an election shall file a report describing the expenditures within 48 hours.

[(B) Additional reports.--After a person files a report under subparagraph (A), the person shall file an additional report within 48 hours after each time the person makes or contracts to make independent expenditures aggregating an additional $10,000 with respect to the same election as that to which the initial report relates.]

(1) Independent expenditures exceeding threshold amount.--

(A) Initial report.--A person (including a political committee) that makes or contracts to make independent expenditures in an aggregate amount equal to or greater than the threshold amount described in paragraph (2) shall electronically file a report describing the expenditures within 24 hours.

(B) Additional reports.--After a person files a report under subparagraph (A), the person shall electronically file an additional report within 24 hours after each time the person makes or contracts to make independent expenditures in an aggregate amount equal to or greater than the threshold amount with respect to the same election as that to which the initial report relates.

(2) Threshold amount described.--In paragraph (1), the ``threshold amount'' means-- (A) during the period up to and including the 20th day before the date of an election, $10,000; or

(B) during the period after the 20th day, but more than 24 hours, before the date of an election, $1,000.

(3) Public availability.--Notwithstanding any other provision of this section, the Commission shall ensure that the information required to be disclosed under this subsection is publicly available through the Commission website not later than 24 hours after receipt in a manner that is downloadable in bulk and machine readable.

* * * * * * *

(5) Disclosure of additional information by covered organizations making payments for public independent expenditures.--

(A) Additional information.--If a covered organization makes or contracts to make public independent expenditures in an aggregate amount equal to or exceeding $10,000 in a calendar year, the report filed by the organization under this subsection shall include, in addition to the information required under paragraph (3), the following information:

(i) If any person made a donation or payment to the covered organization during the covered organization reporting period which was provided for the purpose of being used for campaign- related activity or in response to a solicitation for funds to be used for campaign-related activity--

(I) subject to subparagraph (C), the identification of each person who made such donations or payments in an aggregate amount equal to or exceeding $600 during such period, presented in the order of the aggregate amount of donations or payments made by such persons during such period (with the identification of the person making the largest donation or payment appearing first); and

(II) if any person identified under subclause (I) designated that the donation or payment be used for campaign-related activity with respect to a specific election or in support of a specific candidate, the name of the election or candidate involved, and if any such person designated that the donation or payment be used for a specific public independent expenditure, a description of the expenditure.

(ii) The identification of each person who made unrestricted donor payments to the organization during the covered organization reporting period--

(I) in an aggregate amount equal to or exceeding $600 during such period, if any of the disbursements made by the organization for any of the public independent expenditures which are covered by the report were not made from the organization's Campaign-Related Activity Account under section 326; or

(II) in an aggregate amount equal to or exceeding $6,000 during such period, if the disbursements made by the organization for all of the public independent expenditures which are covered by the report were made exclusively from the organization's Campaign-Related Activity Account under section 326 (but only if the organization has made deposits described in subparagraph (D) of section 326(a)(2) into that Account during such period in an aggregate amount equal to or greater than $10,000), presented in the order of the aggregate amount of payments made by such persons during such period (with the identification of the person making the largest payment appearing first).

(B) Treatment of transfers made to other persons.--

(i) In general.--For purposes of the requirement to file reports under this subsection (including the requirement under subparagraph (A) to include additional information in such reports), a covered organization which transfers amounts to another person (other than the covered organization itself) for the purpose of making a public independent expenditure by that person or by any other person, or (in accordance with clause (ii)) which is deemed to have transferred amounts to another person (other than the covered organization itself) for the purpose of making a public independent expenditure by that person or by any other person, shall be considered to have made a public independent expenditure.

(ii) Rules for deeming transfers made for purpose of making expenditures.-- For purposes of clause (i), in determining whether a covered organization or any other person who transfers amounts to another person shall be deemed to have transferred the amounts for the purpose of making a public independent expenditure, the following rules apply:

(I) The person shall be deemed to have transferred the amounts for the purpose of making a public independent expenditure if--

(aa) the person

designates, requests, or suggests that the amounts be used for public independent expenditures and the person to whom the amounts were transferred agrees to do so or does so;

(bb) the person making the public independent expenditure or another person acting on that person's behalf expressly solicited the person for a donation or payment for making or paying for any public independent expenditures;

(cc) the person and the person to whom the amounts were transferred engaged in substantial written or oral discussion regarding the person either making, or donating or paying for, any public independent expenditures;

(dd) the person or the person to whom the amounts were transferred knew or had reason to know of the covered organization's intent to make public independent expenditures; or

(ee) the person or the person to whom the amounts were transferred made a public independent expenditure during the 2-year period which ends on the date on which the amounts were transferred.

(II) The person shall not be deemed to have transferred the amounts for the purpose of making a public independent expenditure if the transfer was a commercial transaction occurring in the ordinary course of business between the person and the person to whom the amounts were transferred, unless there is affirmative evidence that the amounts were transferred for the purpose of making a public independent expenditure.

(C) Exclusion of amounts designated for other campaign-related activity.--For purposes of subparagraph (A)(i), in determining the amount of a donation or payment made by a person which was provided for the purpose of being used for campaign-related activity or in response to a solicitation for funds to be used for campaign- related activity, there shall be excluded any amount which was designated by the person to be used--

(i) for campaign-related activity described in clause (i) of section 325(d)(2)(A) (relating to independent expenditures) with respect to a different election, or with respect to a candidate in a different election, than an election which is the subject of any of the public independent expenditures covered by the report involved; or

(ii) for any campaign-related activity described in clause (ii) of section 325(d)(2)(A) (relating to electioneering communications).

(D) Exclusion of amounts paid from separate segregated fund.--In determining the amount of public independent expenditures made by a covered organization for purposes of this paragraph, there shall be excluded any amounts paid from a separate segregated fund established and administered by the organization under section 316(b)(2)(C).

(E) Covered organization reporting period described.--In this paragraph, the ``covered organization reporting period'' is, with respect to a report filed by a covered organization under this subsection--

(i) in the case of the first report filed by a covered organization under this subsection which includes information required under this paragraph, the shorter of--

(I) the period which begins on the effective date of the Democracy is Strengthened by Casting Light on Spending in Elections Act and ends on the last day covered by the report,

or

(II) the 12-month period ending on the last day covered by the report; and

(ii) in the case of any subsequent report filed by a covered organization under this subsection which includes information required under this paragraph, the period occurring since the most recent report filed by the organization which includes such information.

(F) Covered organization defined.--In this paragraph, the term ``covered organization'' means any of the following:

(i) Any corporation which is subject to section 316(a).

(ii) Any labor organization (as defined in section 316).

(iii) Any organization described in paragraph (4), (5), or (6) of section 501(c) of the Internal Revenue Code of 1986 and exempt from tax under section 501(a) of such Code.

(iv) Any political organization under section 527 of the Internal Revenue Code of 1986, other than a political committee under this Act.

(G) Other definitions.--In this paragraph--

(i) the terms ``campaign-related activity'' and ``unrestricted donor payment'' have the meaning given such terms in section 325; and

(ii) the term ``public independent expenditure'' means an independent expenditure for a public communication (as defined in section 301(22)).

* * * * * * *

LIMITATIONS ON CONTRIBUTIONS AND EXPENDITURES

Sec. 315. (a) * * *

* * * * * * *

(d)(1) Notwithstanding any other provision of law with respect to limitations on expenditures or limitations on contributions, the national committee of a political party and a State committee of a political party, including any subordinate committee of a State committee, may make expenditures in connection with the general election campaign of candidates for Federal office, subject to the limitations contained in [paragraphs (2), (3), and (4)] paragraphs (2) and (3) of this subsection.

* * * * * * *

[(4) Independent versus coordinated expenditures by party.--

[(A) In general.--On or after the date on which a political party nominates a candidate, no committee of the political party may make--

[(i) any coordinated expenditure under this subsection with respect to the candidate during the election cycle at any time after it makes any independent expenditure (as defined in section 301(17)) with respect to the candidate during the election cycle; or

[(ii) any independent expenditure (as defined in section 301(17)) with respect to the candidate during the election cycle at any time after it makes any coordinated expenditure under this subsection with respect to the candidate during the election cycle.

[(B) Application.--For purposes of this paragraph, all political committees established and maintained by a national political party (including all congressional campaign committees) and all political committees established and maintained by a State political party (including any subordinate committee of a State committee) shall be considered to be a single political committee.

[(C) Transfers.--A committee of a political party that makes coordinated expenditures under this subsection with respect to a candidate shall not, during an election cycle, transfer any funds to, assign authority to make coordinated expenditures under this subsection to, or receive a transfer of funds from, a committee of the political party that has made or intends to make an independent expenditure with respect to the candidate.]

(4) Special Rule for Direct Costs of Communications.--The direct costs incurred by a political committee of a political party for a communication made in connection with the campaign of a candidate for Federal office shall not be subject to the limitations contained in paragraphs (2) and (3) unless the communication is controlled by, or made at the direction of, the candidate or an authorized committee of the candidate.

* * * * * * *

[CONTRIBUTIONS] CONTRIBUTIONS, INDEPENDENT EXPENDITURES, AND ELECTIONEERING COMMUNICATIONS BY GOVERNMENT CONTRACTORS

Sec. 317. (a) It shall be unlawful for any person--

(1) who enters into any contract with the United States or any department or agency thereof either for the rendition of personal services or furnishing any material, supplies, or equipment to the United States or any department or agency thereof or for selling any land or building to the United States or any department or agency thereof, if payment for the performance of such contract or payment for such material, supplies, equipment, land, or building is to be made in whole or in part from funds appropriated by the Congress, at any time between the commencement of negotiations for and the later of (A) the completion of performance under;

or (B) the termination of negotiations for, such contract or furnishing of material, supplies, equipment, land, or buildings, directly or indirectly to make any contribution of money or other things of value, or to promise expressly or impliedly to make any such contribution to any political party, committee, or candidate for public office or to any person for any political [purpose or use; or] purpose or use, to make any independent expenditure, or to disburse any funds for an electioneering communication;

(2) who enters into negotiations for financial assistance under title I of the Emergency Economic Stabilization Act of 2008 (12 U.S.C. 5211 et seq.) (relating to the purchase of troubled assets by the Secretary of the Treasury), during the period--

(A) beginning on the later of the commencement of the negotiations or the date of the enactment of the Democracy is Strengthened by Casting Light on Spending in Elections Act; and

(B) ending with the later of the termination of such negotiations or the repayment of such financial assistance; directly or indirectly to make any contribution of money or other things of value, or to promise expressly or impliedly to make any such contribution to any political party, committee, or candidate for public office or to any person for any political purpose or use, to make any independent expenditure, or to disburse any funds for an electioneering communication; or

[(2)] (3) knowingly to solicit any such contribution from any such person for any such purpose during any such period.

(b) To the extent that subsection (a)(1) prohibits a person who enters into a contract described in such subsection from making any independent expenditure or disbursing funds for an electioneering communication, such subsection shall apply only if the value of the contract is equal to or greater than $7,000,000.

[(b)] (c) This section does not prohibit or make unlawful the establishment or administration of, or the solicitation of contributions to, any separate segregated fund by any corporation, labor organization, membership organization, cooperative, or corporation without capital stock for the purpose of influencing the nomination for election, or election, of any person to Federal office, unless the provisions of [section 321] section 316 prohibit or make unlawful the establishment or administration of, or the solicitation of contributions to, such fund. Each specific prohibition, allowance, and duty applicable to a corporation, labor organization, or separate segregated fund under [section 321] section 316 applies to a corporation, labor organization, or separate segregated fund to which this subsection applies.

[(c)] (d) For purposes of this section, the term ``labor organization'' has the meaning given it by [section 321] section 316(b)(1).

PUBLICATION AND DISTRIBUTION OF STATEMENTS AND SOLICITATIONS

Sec. 318. (a) Whenever a political committee makes a disbursement for the purpose of financing any communication through any broadcasting station, newspaper, magazine, outdoor advertising facility, mailing, or any other type of general public political advertising, or whenever any person makes a disbursement [for the purpose of financing communications expressly advocating the election or defeat of a clearly identified candidate] for an independent expenditure consisting of a public communication, or solicits any contribution through any broadcasting station, newspaper, magazine, outdoor advertising facility, mailing, or any other type of general public political advertising or makes a disbursement for an electioneering communication (as defined in section 304(f)(3)), such communication-- (1) * * *

* * * * * * *

[(3) if not authorized by a candidate, an authorized political committee of a candidate, or its agents, shall clearly state the name and permanent street address, telephone number, or World Wide Web address of the person who paid for the communication and state that the communication is not authorized by any candidate or candidate's committee.]

(3) if not authorized by a candidate, an authorized political committee of a candidate, or its agents, shall clearly state--

(A) the name and permanent street address, telephone number, or World Wide Web address of the person who paid for the communication;

(B) if the communication is an independent expenditure consisting of a mass mailing (as defined in section 301(23)) which is paid for in whole or in part with a payment which is treated as a disbursement by a covered organization for campaign-related activity under section 325, the name and permanent street address, telephone number, or World Wide Web address of--

(I) the significant funder of the communication, if any (as determined in accordance with subsection (e)(4)(C)(i)); and

(ii) each person who would be included in the Top 5 Funders list which would be submitted with respect to the communication if the communication were transmitted through television, if any (as determined in accordance with subsection (e)(5)); and

(C) that the communication is not authorized by any candidate or candidate's committee.

* * * * * * *

(d) Additional Requirements.--

(1) * * *

(2) Communications by [others] political

committees.--Any communication described in paragraph (3) of [subsection (a)] subsection (a) which is paid for by a political committee (including a political committee of a political party), other than a political committee which makes only electioneering communications or independent expenditures consisting of public communications, which is transmitted through radio or television shall include, in addition to the requirements of that paragraph, in a clearly spoken manner, the following audio statement: ``_____ is responsible for the content of this advertising." (with the blank to be filled in with the name of the political committee [or other person] paying for the communication and the name of any connected organization of the payor). If transmitted through television, the statement shall be conveyed by an unobscured, full-screen view of a representative of the political committee [or other person] making the statement, or by a representative of such political committee [or other person] in voice-over, and shall also appear in a clearly readable manner with a reasonable degree of color contrast between the background and the printed statement, for a period of at least 4 seconds.

(e) Communications by Others.--

(1) In general.--Any communication described in paragraph (3) of subsection (a) which is transmitted through radio or television (other than a communication to which subsection (d)(2) applies because the communication is paid for by a political committee, including a political committee of a political party, other than a political committee which makes only electioneering communications or independent expenditures consisting of public communications) shall include, in addition to the requirements of that paragraph, the following:

(A) The individual disclosure statement described in paragraph (2) (if the person paying for the communication is an individual) or the organizational disclosure statement described in paragraph (3) (if the person paying for the communication is not an individual).

(B) If the communication is an electioneering communication or an independent expenditure consisting of a public communication and is paid for in whole or in part with a payment which is treated as a disbursement by a covered organization for campaign-related activity under section 325, the significant funder disclosure statement described in paragraph (4) (if applicable), unless, on the basis of criteria established in regulations promulgated by the Commission, the communication is of such short duration that including the statement in the communication would constitute a hardship to the person paying for the communication by requiring a disproportionate amount of the communication's content to consist of the statement.

(C) If the communication is an electioneering communication or an independent expenditure consisting of a public communication and is paid for in whole or in part with a payment which is treated as a disbursement by a covered organization for campaign-related activity under section 325, the Top Five Funders list described in paragraph (5) (if applicable), unless, on the basis of criteria established in regulations promulgated by the Commission, the communication is of such short duration that including the Top Five Funders list in the communication would constitute a hardship to the person paying for the communication by requiring a disproportionate amount of the communication's content to consist of the Top Five Funders list.

(2) Individual disclosure statement described.--The individual disclosure statement described in this paragraph is the following: ``I am _______, and I approve this message.'', with the blank filled in with the name of the applicable individual.

(3) Organizational disclosure statement described.--

The organizational disclosure statement described in this paragraph is the following: ``I am _______, the _______ of _______, and _______ approves this message.'', with--

(A) the first blank to be filled in with the name of the applicable individual;

(B) the second blank to be filled in with the title of the applicable individual; and

(C) the third and fourth blank each to be filled in with the name of the organization or other person paying for the communication.

(4) Significant funder disclosure statement described.--

(A) Statement if significant funder is an individual.--If the significant funder of a communication paid for in whole or in part with a payment which is treated as a disbursement by a covered organization for campaign-related activity under section 325 is an individual, the significant funder disclosure statement described in this paragraph is the following:

``I am _______. I helped to pay for this message, and I approve it.'', with the blank filled in with the name of the applicable individual.

(B) Statement if significant funder is not an individual.--If the significant funder of a communication paid for in whole or in part with a payment which is treated as a disbursement by a covered organization for campaign-related activity under section 325 is not an individual, the significant funder disclosure statement described in this paragraph is the following: ``I am _______, the _______ of

_______. _______ helped to pay for this message, and _______ approves it.'', with--

(i) the first blank to be filled in with the name of the applicable individual;

(ii) the second blank to be filled in with the title of the applicable individual; and

(iii) the third, fourth, and fifth blank each to be filled in with the name of the significant funder of the communication.

(C) Significant funder defined.--

(i) Independent expenditures.--For purposes of this paragraph, the ``significant funder'' with respect to an independent expenditure consisting of a public communication paid for in whole or in part with a payment which is treated as a disbursement by a covered organization for campaign- related activity under section 325 shall be determined as follows:

(I) If any report filed by any organization with respect to the independent expenditure under section 304 includes information on any person who made a payment to the organization in an amount equal to or exceeding $100,000 which was designated by the person to be used for campaign-related activity consisting of that specific independent expenditure (as required to be included in the report under section 304(g)(5)(A)(i)), the person who is identified among all such reports as making the largest such payment.

(II) If any report filed by any organization with respect to the independent expenditure under section 304 includes information on any person who made a payment to the organization in an amount equal to or exceeding $100,000 which was designated by the person to be used for campaign-related activity with respect to the same election or in support of the same candidate (as required to be included in the report under section 304(g)(5)(A)(i)) but subclause (I) does not apply, the person who is identified among all such reports as making the largest such payment.

(III) If any report filed by any organization with respect to the independent expenditure under section 304 includes information on any person who made a payment to the organization which was provided for the purpose of being used for campaign-related activity or in response to a solicitation for funds to be used for campaign-related activity (as required to be included in the report under section 304(g)(5)(A)(i)) but subclause (I) or subclause (II) does not apply, the person who is identified among all such reports as making the largest such payment.

(IV) If none of the reports filed by any organization with respect to the independent expenditure under section 304 includes information on any person (other than the organization) who made a payment to the organization which was provided for the purpose of being used for campaign-related activity or in response to a solicitation for funds to be used for campaign- related activity, but any of such reports includes information on any person who made an unrestricted donor payment to the organization (as required to be included in the report under section 304(g)(5)(A)(ii)), the person who is identified among all such reports as making the largest such unrestricted donor payment.

(ii) Electioneering communications.--

For purposes of this paragraph, the ``significant funder'' with respect to an electioneering communication paid for in whole or in part with a payment which is treated as a disbursement by a covered organization for campaign- related activity under section 325, shall be determined as follows:

(I) If any report filed by any organization with respect to the electioneering communication under section 304 includes information on any person who made a payment to the organization in an amount equal to or exceeding $100,000 which was designated by the person to be used for campaign- related activity consisting of that specific electioneering communication (as required to be included in the report under section 304(f)(6)(A)(i)), the person who is identified among all such reports as making the largest such payment.

(II) If any report filed by any organization with respect to the electioneering communication under section 304 includes information on any person who made a payment to the organization in an amount equal to or exceeding $100,000 which was designated by the person to be used for campaign- related activity with respect to the same election or in support of the same candidate (as required to be included in the report under section 304(f)(6)(A)(i)) but subclause (I) does not apply, the person who is identified among all such reports as making the largest such payment.

(III) If any report filed by any organization with respect to the electioneering communication under section 304 includes information on any person who made a payment to the organization which was provided for the purpose of being used for campaign-related activity or in response to a solicitation for funds to be used for campaign-related activity (as required to be included in the report under section 304(f)(6)(A)(i)) but subclause (I) or subclause (II) does not apply, the person who is identified among all such reports as making the largest such payment.

(IV) If none of the reports filed by any organization with respect to the electioneering communication under section 304 includes information on any person who made a payment to the organization which was provided for the purpose of being used for campaign-related activity or in response to a solicitation for funds to be used for campaign-related activity, but any of such reports includes information on any person who made an unrestricted donor payment to the organization (as required to be included in the report under section 304(f)(6)(A)(ii)), the person who is identified among all such reports as making the largest such unrestricted donor payment.

(5) Top 5 funders list described.--With respect to a communication paid for in whole or in part with a payment which is treated as a disbursement by a covered organization for campaign-related activity under section 325, the Top 5 Funders list described in this paragraph is--

(A) in the case of a disbursement for an independent expenditure consisting of a public communication, a list of the 5 persons (or, in the case of a communication transmitted through radio, the 2 persons) who provided the largest payments of any type which are required under section 304(g)(5)(A) to be included in the reports filed by any organization with respect to that independent expenditure under section 304, together with the amount of the payments each such person provided; or

(B) in the case of a disbursement for an electioneering communication, a list of the 5 persons (or, in the case of a communication transmitted through radio, the 2 persons) who provided the largest payments of any type which are required under section 304(f)(6)(A) to be included in the reports filed by any organization with respect to that electioneering communication under section 304, together with the amount of the payments each such person provided.

(6) Method of conveyance of statement.--

(A) Communications transmitted through radio.--In the case of a communication to which this subsection applies which is transmitted through radio, the disclosure statements required under paragraph (1) shall be made by audio by the applicable individual in a clearly spoken manner.

(B) Communications transmitted through television.--In the case of a communication to which this subsection applies which is transmitted through television, the information required under paragraph (1)--

(i) shall appear in writing at the end of the communication in a clearly readable manner, with a reasonable degree of color contrast between the background and the printed statement, for a period of at least 6 seconds; and

(ii) except in the case of a Top 5 Funders list described in paragraph (5), shall also be conveyed by an unobscured, full-screen view of the applicable individual, or by the applicable individual making the statement in voice-over accompanied by a clearly identifiable photograph or similar image of the individual.

(7) Applicable individual defined.--In this subsection, the term ``applicable individual'' means, with respect to a communication to which this paragraph applies--

(A) if the communication is paid for by an individual or if the significant funder of the communication under paragraph (4) is an individual, the individual involved;

(B) if the communication is paid for by a corporation or if the significant funder of the communication under paragraph (4) is a corporation, the chief executive officer of the corporation (or, if the corporation does not have a chief executive officer, the highest ranking official of the corporation);

(C) if the communication is paid for by a labor organization or if the significant funder of the communication under paragraph (4) is a labor organization, the highest ranking officer of the labor organization; or

(D) if the communication is paid for by any other person or if the significant funder of the communication under paragraph (4) is any other person, the highest ranking official of such person.

(8) Covered organization defined.--In this subsection, the term ``covered organization'' means any of the following:

(A) Any corporation which is subject to section 316(a).

(B) Any labor organization (as defined in section 316).

(C) Any organization described in paragraph (4), (5), or (6) of section 501(c) of the Internal Revenue Code of 1986 and exempt from tax under section 501(a) of such Code.

(D) Any political organization under section 527 of the Internal Revenue Code of 1986, other than a political committee under this Act.

(9) Other definitions.--In this subsection, the terms ``campaign-related activity'' and ``unrestricted donor payment'' have the meaning given such terms in section 325.

(f) Special Rules for Political Robocalls.--

(1) Requiring communications to include certain disclaimer statements.--Any communication consisting of a political robocall which would be subject to the requirements of subsection (e) if the communication were transmitted through radio or television shall include the following:

(A) The individual disclosure statement described in subsection (e)(2) (if the person paying for the communication is an individual) or the organizational disclosure statement described in subsection (e)(3) (if the person paying for the communication is not an individual).

(B) If the communication is an electioneering communication or an independent expenditure consisting of a public communication and is paid for in whole or in part with a payment which is treated as a disbursement by a covered organization for campaign-related activity under section 325, the significant funder disclosure statement described in subsection (e)(4) (if applicable).

(2) Timing of certain statement.--The statement required to be included under paragraph (1)(A) shall be made at the beginning of the political robocall.

(3) Political robocall defined.--In this subsection, the term ``political robocall'' means any outbound telephone call--

(A) in which a person is not available to speak with the person answering the call, and the call instead plays a recorded message; and (B) which promotes, supports, attacks, or opposes a candidate for election for Federal office.

CONTRIBUTIONS AND DONATIONS BY FOREIGN NATIONALS

Sec. 319. (a) * * *

(b) As used in this section, the term ``foreign national'' means--

(1) a foreign principal, as such term is defined by section 1(b) of the Foreign Agents Registration Act of 1938 (22 U.S.C. 611(b)), except that the term ``foreign national'' shall not include any individual who is a citizen of the United States; [or]

(2) an individual who is not a citizen of the United States or a national of the United States (as defined in section 101(a)(22) of the Immigration and Nationality Act) and who is not lawfully admitted for permanent residence, as defined by section 101(a)(20) of the Immigration and Nationality Act (8 U.S.C. 1101(a)(20))[.]; or

(3) any corporation which is not a foreign national described in paragraph (1) and--

(A) in which a foreign national described in paragraph (1) or (2) directly or indirectly owns 20 percent or more of the voting shares;

(B) with respect to which the majority of the members of the board of directors are foreign nationals described in paragraph (1) or (2);

(C) over which one or more foreign nationals described in paragraph (1) or (2) has the power to direct, dictate, or control the decision- making process of the corporation with respect to its interests in the United States; or

(D) over which one or more foreign nationals described in paragraph (1) or (2) has the power to direct, dictate, or control the decision- making process of the corporation with respect to activities in connection with a Federal, State, or local election, including--

(i) the making of a contribution, donation, expenditure, independent expenditure, or disbursement for an electioneering communication (within the meaning of section 304(f)(3)); or

(ii) the administration of a political committee established or maintained by the corporation.

(c) Certification of Compliance Required Prior to Carrying Out Activity.--Prior to the making in connection with an election for Federal office of any contribution, donation, expenditure, independent expenditure, or disbursement for an electioneering communication by a corporation during a year, the chief executive officer of the corporation (or, if the corporation does not have a chief executive officer, the highest ranking official of the corporation), shall file a certification with the Commission, under penalty of perjury, that the corporation is not prohibited from carrying out such activity under subsection (b)(3), unless the chief executive officer has previously filed such a certification during the year. Nothing in this subsection shall be construed to apply to any contribution, donation, expenditure, independent expenditure, or disbursement from a separate segregated fund established and administered by a corporation under section 316(b)(2)(C).

(d) No Effect on Separate Segregate Funds of Domestic Corporations.--Nothing in this section shall be construed to prohibit any corporation which is not a foreign national described in paragraph (1) of subsection (b) from establishing, administering, and soliciting contributions to a separate segregated fund under section 316(b)(2)(C), so long as none of the amounts in the fund are provided by any foreign national described in paragraph (1) or (2) of subsection (b) and no foreign national described in paragraph (1) or (2) of subsection (b) has the power to direct, dictate, or control the establishment or administration of the fund.

(e) No Effect on Other Laws.--Nothing in this section shall be construed to affect the determination of whether a corporation is treated as a foreign national for purposes of any law other than this Act.

* * * * * * *

PROHIBITION OF CONTRIBUTIONS BY MINORS

[Sec. 324. An individual who is 17 years old or younger shall not make a contribution to a candidate or a contribution or donation to a committee of a political party.]

Sec. 324. Coordinated Communications.

(a) Coordinated Communications Defined.--For purposes of this Act, the term ``coordinated communication'' means--

(1) a covered communication which, subject to subsection (c), is made in cooperation, consultation, or concert with, or at the request or suggestion of, a candidate, an authorized committee of a candidate, or a political committee of a political party; or

(2) any communication that republishes, disseminates, or distributes, in whole or in part, any broadcast or any written, graphic, or other form of campaign material prepared by a candidate, an authorized committee of a candidate, or their agents.

(b) Covered Communication Defined.--

(1) In general.--Except as provided in paragraph (4), for purposes of this subsection, the term ``covered communication'' means, for purposes of the applicable election period described in paragraph (2), a public communication (as defined in section 301(22)) that refers to a clearly identified candidate for Federal office and is publicly distributed or publicly disseminated during such period.

(2) Applicable election period.--For purposes of paragraph (1), the ``applicable election period'' with respect to a communication means--

(A) in the case of a communication which refers to a candidate for the office of President or Vice President, the period--

(i) beginning with the date that is 120 days before the date of the first primary election, preference election, or nominating convention for nomination for the office of President which is held in any State; and

(ii) ending with the date of the general election for such office; or

(B) in the case of a communication which refers to a candidate for any other Federal office, the period--

(i) beginning with the date that is 90 days before the earliest of the primary election, preference election, or nominating convention with respect to the nomination for the office that the candidate is seeking; and

(ii) ending with the date of the general election for such office.

(3) Special rule for public distribution of communications involving congressional candidates.--For purposes of paragraph (1), in the case of a communication involving a candidate for an office other than President or Vice President, the communication shall be considered to be publicly distributed or publicly disseminated only if the dissemination or distribution occurs in the jurisdiction of the office that the candidate is seeking.

(4) Exception.--The term ``covered communication" does not include--

(A) a communication appearing in a news story, commentary, or editorial distributed through the facilities of any broadcasting station, newspaper, magazine, or other periodical publication, unless such facilities are owned or controlled by any political party, political committee, or candidate; or

(B) a communication which constitutes a candidate debate or forum conducted pursuant to the regulations adopted by the Commission to carry out section 304(f)(3)(B)(iii), or which solely promotes such a debate or forum and is made by or on behalf of the person sponsoring the debate or forum.

(c) No Finding of Coordination Based Solely on Sharing of Information Regarding Legislative or Policy Position.--For purposes of subsection (a)(1), a covered communication may not be considered to be made in cooperation, consultation, or concert with, or at the request or suggestion of, a candidate, an authorized committee of a candidate, or a political committee of a political party solely on the grounds that a person provided information to the candidate or committee regarding that person's position on a legislative or policy matter (including urging the candidate or party to adopt that person's position), so long as there is no discussion between the person and the candidate or committee regarding the candidate's campaign for election for Federal office.

(d) Preservation of Certain Safe Harbors and Firewalls.--

Nothing in this section may be construed to affect 11 CFR 109.21(g) or (h), as in effect on the date of the enactment of the Democracy is Strengthened by Casting Light on Spending in Elections Act.

(e) Treatment of Coordination With Political Parties for Communications Referring to Candidates.--For purposes of this section, if a communication which refers to any clearly identified candidate or candidates of a political party or any opponent of such a candidate or candidates is determined to have been made in cooperation, consultation, or concert with or at the request or suggestion of a political committee of the political party but not in cooperation, consultation, or concert with or at the request or suggestion of such clearly identified candidate or candidates, the communication shall be treated as having been made in cooperation, consultation, or concert with or at the request or suggestion of the political committee of the political party but not with or at the request or suggestion of such clearly identified candidate or candidates.

Sec. 325. Special Rules for Use of General Treasury Funds by Covered Organizations for Campaign-Related Activity.

(a) Use of Funds for Campaign-Related Activity.--

(1) In general.--Subject to any applicable restrictions and prohibitions under this Act, a covered organization may make disbursements for campaign- related activity using--

(A) amounts paid or donated to the organization which are designated by the person providing the amounts to be used for campaign- related activity;

(B) unrestricted donor payments made to the organization; and

(C) other funds of the organization, including amounts received pursuant to commercial activities in the regular course of a covered organization's business.

(2) No effect on use of separate segregated fund.-- Nothing in this section shall be construed to affect the authority of a covered organization to make disbursements from a separate segregated fund established and administered by the organization under section 316(b)(2)(C).

(b) Mutually Agreed Restrictions on Use of Funds for Campaign-Related Activity.--

(1) Agreement and certification.--If a covered organization and a person mutually agree, at the time the person makes a donation, payment, or transfer to the organization which would require the organization to disclose the person's identification under section 304(g)(5)(A)(ii) or section 304(f)(6)(A)(ii), that the organization will not use the donation, payment, or transfer for campaign-related activity, then not later than 30 days after the organization receives the donation, payment, or transfer the organization shall transmit to the person a written certification by the chief financial officer of the covered organization (or, if the organization does not have a chief financial officer, the highest ranking financial official of the organization) that--

(A) the organization will not use the donation, payment, or transfer for campaign- related activity; and

(B) the organization will not include any information on the person in any report filed by the organization under section 304 with respect to independent expenditures or electioneering communications, so that the person will not be required to appear in a significant funder statement or a Top 5 Funders list under section 318(e).

(2) Exception for payments made pursuant to commercial activities.--Paragraph (1) does not apply with respect to any payment or transfer made pursuant to commercial activities in the regular course of a covered organization's business.

(c) Certifications Regarding Disbursements for Campaign-Related Activity.--

(1) Certification by chief executive officer.--If, at any time during a calendar quarter, a covered organization makes a disbursement of funds for campaign-related activity using funds described in subsection (a)(1), the chief executive officer of the covered organization or the chief executive officer's designee (or, if the organization does not have a chief executive officer, the highest ranking official of the organization or the highest ranking official's designee) shall file a statement with the Commission which contains the following certifications:

(A) None of the campaign-related activity for which the organization disbursed the funds during the quarter was made in cooperation, consultation, or concert with, or at the request or suggestion of, any candidate or any authorized committee or agent of such candidate, or political committee of a political party or agent of any political party.

(B) The chief executive officer or highest ranking official of the covered organization (as the case may be) has reviewed and approved each statement and report filed by the organization under section 304 with respect to any such disbursement made during the quarter.

(C) Each statement and report filed by the organization under section 304 with respect to any such disbursement made during the quarter is complete and accurate.

(D) All such disbursements made during the quarter are in compliance with this Act.

(E) No portion of the amounts used to make any such disbursements during the quarter is attributable to funds received by the organization that were restricted by the person who provided the funds from being used for campaign-related activity pursuant to subsection (b).

(2) Application of electronic filing rules.--Section 304(d)(1) shall apply with respect to a statement required under this subsection in the same manner as such section applies with respect to a statement under subsection (c) or (g) of section 304.

(3) Deadline.--The chief executive officer or highest ranking official of a covered organization (as the case may be) shall file the statement required under this subsection with respect to a calendar quarter not later than 15 days after the end of the quarter.

(d) Definitions.--For purposes of this section, the following definitions apply:

(1) Covered organization.--The term ``covered organization'' means any of the following:

(A) Any corporation which is subject to section 316(a).

(B) Any labor organization (as defined in section 316).

(C) Any organization described in paragraph (4), (5), or (6) of section 501(c) of the Internal Revenue Code of 1986 and exempt from tax under section 501(a) of such Code.

(D) Any political organization under section 527 of the Internal Revenue Code of 1986, other than a political committee under this Act.

(2) Campaign-related activity.--

(A) In general.--The term ``campaign-related activity'' means--

(i) an independent expenditure consisting of a public communication (as defined in section 301(22)), a transfer of funds to another person (other than the transferor itself) for the purpose of making such an independent expenditure by that person or by any other person, or (in accordance with subparagraph (B)) a transfer of funds to another person (other than the transferor itself) which is deemed to have been made for the purpose of making such an independent expenditure by that person or by any other person; or

(ii) an electioneering communication, a transfer of funds to another person (other than the transferor itself) for the purpose of making an electioneering communication by that person or by any other person, or (in accordance with subparagraph (B)) a transfer of funds to another person (other than the transferor itself)which is deemed to have been made for the purpose of making an electioneering communication by that person or by any other person.

(B) Rule for deeming transfers made for purpose of campaign-related activity.--For purposes of subparagraph (A), in determining whether a transfer of funds by one person to another person shall be deemed to have been made for the purpose of making an independent expenditure consisting of a public communication or an electioneering communication, the following rules apply:

(i) The transfer shall be deemed to have been made for the purpose of making such an independent expenditure or an electioneering communication if--

(I) the person designates, requests, or suggests that the amounts be used for such independent expenditures or electioneering communications and the person to whom the amounts were transferred agrees to do so or does so;

(II) the person making such independent expenditures or electioneering communications or another person acting on that person's behalf expressly solicited the person for a donation or payment for making or paying for any such independent expenditure or electioneering communication;

(III) the person and the person to whom the amounts were transferred engaged in substantial written or oral discussion regarding the person either making, or donating or paying for, such independent expenditures or electioneering communications;

(IV) the person or the person to whom the amounts were transferred knew or had reason to know of the covered organization's intent to disburse funds for such independent expenditures or electioneering communications;

or

(V) the person or the person to whom the amounts were transferred made such an independent expenditure or electioneering communication during the 2-year period which ends on the date on which the amounts were transferred.

(ii) The transfer shall not be deemed to have been made for the purpose of making such an independent expenditure or an electioneering communication if the transfer was a commercial transaction occurring in the ordinary course of business between the person and the person to whom the amounts were transferred, unless there is affirmative evidence that the amounts were transferred for the purpose of making such an independent expenditure or electioneering communication.

(3) Unrestricted donor payment.--The term ``unrestricted donor payment'' means a payment to a covered organization which consists of a donation or payment from a person other than the covered organization, except that such term does not include--

(A) any payment made pursuant to commercial activities in the regular course of a covered organization's business; or

(B) any donation or payment which is designated by the person making the donation or payment to be used for campaign-related activity or made in response to a solicitation for funds to be used for campaign-related activity.

SEC. 326. OPTIONAL USE OF SEPARATE ACCOUNT BY COVERED ORGANIZATIONS FOR CAMPAIGN-RELATED ACTIVITY

(a) Optional Use of Separate Account.--

(1) Establishment of account.--

(A) In general.--At its option, a covered organization may make disbursements for campaign-related activity using amounts from a bank account established and controlled by the organization to be known as the Campaign- Related Activity Account (hereafter in this section referred to as the ``Account''), which shall be maintained separately from all other accounts of the organization and which shall consist exclusively of the deposits described in paragraph (2).

(B) Mandatory use of account after establishment.--If a covered organization establishes an Account under this section, it may not make disbursements for campaign-related activity from any source other than amounts from the Account.

(C) Exclusive use of account for campaign- related activity.--Amounts in the Account shall be used exclusively for disbursements by the covered organization for campaign-related activity. After such disbursements are made, information with respect to deposits made to the Account shall be disclosed in accordance with section 304(g)(5) or section 304(f)(6).

(2) Deposits described.--The deposits described in this paragraph are deposits of the following amounts:

(A) Amounts donated or paid to the covered organization by a person other than the organization for the purpose of being used for campaign-related activity, and for which the person providing the amounts has designated that the amounts be used for campaign-related activity with respect to a specific election or specific candidate.

(B) Amounts donated or paid to the covered organization by a person other than the organization for the purpose of being used for campaign-related activity, and for which the person providing the amounts has not designated that the amounts be used for campaign-related activity with respect to a specific election or specific candidate.

(C) Amounts donated or paid to the covered organization by a person other than the organization in response to a solicitation for funds to be used for campaign-related activity.

(D) Amounts transferred to the Account by the covered organization from other accounts of the organization, including from the organization's general treasury funds.

(3) No treatment as political committee.--The establishment and administration of an Account in accordance with this subsection shall not by itself be treated as the establishment or administration of a political committee for any purpose of this Act.

(b) Reduction in Amounts Otherwise Available for Account in Response to Demand of General Donors.--

(1) In general.--If a covered organization which has established an Account obtains any revenues during a year which are attributable to a donation or payment from a person other than the covered organization, and if any person who makes such a donation or payment to the organization notifies the organization in writing (at the time of making the donation or payment) that the organization may not use the donation or payment for campaign-related activity, the organization shall reduce the amount of its revenues available for deposits to the Account which are described in subsection (a)(3)(D) during the year by the amount of the donation or payment.

(2) Exception.--Paragraph (1) does not apply with respect to any payment made pursuant to commercial activities in the regular course of a covered organization's business.

(c) Covered Organization Defined.--In this section, the term ``covered organization'' means any of the following:

(1) Any corporation which is subject to section 316(a).

(2) Any labor organization (as defined in section 316).

(3) Any organization described in paragraph (4), (5), or (6) of section 501(c) of the Internal Revenue Code of 1986 and exempt from tax under section 501(a) of such Code.

(4) Any political organization under section 527 of the Internal Revenue Code of 1986, other than a political committee under this Act.

(d) Campaign-Related Activity Defined.--In this section, the term ``campaign-related activity'' has the meaning given such term in section 325.

Sec. 327. Disclosures by Covered Organizations to Shareholders, Members, and Donors of Information on Disbursements for Campaign-Related Activity

(a) Including Information in Regular Periodic Reports.--

(1) In general.--A covered organization which submits regular, periodic reports to its shareholders, members, or donors on its finances or activities shall include in each such report the information described in paragraph (2) with respect to the disbursements made by the organization for campaign-related activity during the period covered by the report.

(2) Information described.--The information described in this paragraph is, for each disbursement for campaign-related activity--

(A) the date of the independent expenditure or electioneering communication involved;

(B) the amount of the independent expenditure or electioneering communication involved;

(C) the name of the candidate identified in the independent expenditure or electioneering communication involved, the office sought by the candidate, and (if applicable) whether the independent expenditure or electioneering communication involved was in support of or in opposition to the candidate;

(D) in the case of a transfer of funds to another person, the information required by subparagraphs (A) through (C), as well as the name of the recipient of the funds and the date and amount of the funds transferred;

(E) the source of such funds; and

(F) such other information as the Commission determines is appropriate to further the purposes of this subsection.

(b) Hyperlink to Information Included in Reports Filed With Commission.--

(1) Requiring posting of hyperlink.--If a covered organization maintains an Internet site, the organization shall post on such Internet site a hyperlink from its homepage to the location on the Internet site of the Commission which contains the following information:

(A) The information the organization is required to report under section 304(g)(5)(A) with respect to public independent expenditures.

(B) The information the organization is required to include in a statement of disbursements for electioneering communications under section 304(f)(6).

(2) Deadline; duration of posting.--The covered organization shall post the hyperlink described in paragraph (1) not later than 24 hours after the Commission posts the information described in such paragraph on the Internet site of the Commission, and shall ensure that the hyperlink remains on the Internet site of the covered organization until the expiration of the 1-year period which begins on the date of the election with respect to which the public independent expenditures or electioneering communications are made.

(c) Covered Organization Defined.--In this section, the term ``covered organization'' means any of the following:

(1) Any corporation which is subject to section 316(a).

(2) Any labor organization (as defined in section 316).

(3) Any organization described in paragraph (4), (5), or (6) of section 501(c) of the Internal Revenue Code of 1986 and exempt from tax under section 501(a) of such Code.

(4) Any political organization under section 527 of the Internal Revenue Code of 1986, other than a political committee under this Act.

* * * * * * *

Lobbying Disclosure Act of 1995

* * * * * * *

Sec. 5. Reports by Registered Lobbyists

(a) * * *

* * * * * * *

(d) Semiannual Reports on Certain Contributions.--

(1) In general.--Not later than 30 days after the end of the semiannual period beginning on the first day of January and July of each year, or on the first business day after such 30th day if the 30th day is not a business day, each person or organization who is registered or is required to register under paragraph (1) or (2) of section 4(a), and each employee who is or is required to be listed as a lobbyist under section 4(b)(6) or subsection (b)(2)(C) of this section, shall file a report with the Secretary of the Senate and the Clerk of the House of Representatives containing--

(A) * * *

* * * * * * *

(F) the name of each Presidential library foundation, and each Presidential inaugural committee, to whom contributions equal to or exceeding $200 were made by the person or organization, or a political committee established or controlled by the person or organization, within the semiannual period, and the date and amount of each such contribution within the semiannual period; [and]

(G) the amount of any independent expenditure (as defined in section 301(17) of the Federal Election Campaign Act of 1971 (2 U.S.C. 431(17)) equal to or greater than $1,000 made by such person or organization, and for each such expenditure the name of each candidate being supported or opposed and the amount spent supporting or opposing each such candidate;

(H) the amount of any electioneering communication (as defined in section 304(f)(3) of such Act (2 U.S.C. 434(f)(3)) equal to or greater than $1,000 made by such person or organization, and for each such communication the name of the candidate referred to in the communication and whether the communication involved was in support of or in opposition to the candidate; and [(G)] (I) a certification by the person or organization filing the report that the person or organization--

(i) * * *

* * * * * * *

MINORITY VIEWS OF REPRESENTATIVES DAN LUNGREN, KEVIN MCCARTHY, AND GREGG HARPER

We find no basis for the proposition that, in the context of political speech, the Government may impose restrictions on certain disfavored speakers.

INTRODUCTION

This bill is nothing less--and nothing more--than an attempt to change the laws of campaign finance to silence the critics of one party in order to give it an advantage over the other. Worse still, the bill is specifically intended to curtail speech before its provisions can be challenged or even understood. The haste of efforts to enact it, the proliferation of errors or miscalculations in its drafting, and the utterly partisan nature of its design betray that this bill is not about good government--it is about protecting the majority's candidates from criticism in the 2010 election.

After a three-month drafting process, Democrats insisted on rushing this bill from introduction (April 29) to hearings (May 6 and 11) to markup (May 20). It appears floor consideration will be equally rushed, perhaps occurring May 27 or 28 (no doubt under the kind of highly restrictive rule that has become the norm in this Congress). This is despite the bill's complexity--it began as an 84-page revision to a system that already regulates 33 types of contributions and speech and 71 different types of speakers, and has only grown. It is despite opposition manifested in letters to the committee from (1) eight former FEC commissioners, (2) a group of more than 85 organizations from a wide range of industries and interests, (3) the Chamber of Commerce, (4) the American Society of Association Executives, (5) the Organization for International Investment, and (6) the Center for Competitive Politics. And it is despite the absence of meaningful bipartisan collaboration or support.

THE RUSH TO PASS

Immediately after the Supreme Court issued its decision in Citizens United v. Federal Election Commission on January 21, 2010, Democrats assigned the chair of their House campaign committee to lead the effort to pass a campaign finance bill (working in collaboration with the former chair of their Senate campaign committee). The sponsors have made clear from the beginning that: (1) they intend for this bill to affect the 2010 elections, and (2) they expect and desire that this bill will deter political speech.

In Citizens United, the Court held that political speech could not be banned based on the corporate form of the speaker.

The practical effect of the ruling is that organizations such as corporations, labor unions, trade associations and nonprofit advocacy groups receiving corporate funds may use their general treasuries (as opposed to their connected PACs) to directly advocate for and against federal candidates. (Contrary to some reports, the decision did not allow corporations to make direct contributions to candidates.)

Despite the breathless rhetoric that began the moment the Court announced its decision, there is no evidence before this Committee (or anywhere else that we can find) showing a change in political spending practices caused by Citizens United. The frantic rush to legislate is not a response to actual facts. It is, instead, an effort to use the Citizens United case as a smokescreen to cover up a historically unprecedented twisting of the campaign finance laws for partisan advantage.

It is no wonder, then, that the bill's advocates prefer to talk about almost anything except what the bill actually says and what it actually will do. Indeed, over the course of two hearings this Committee heard from only one witness--the general counsel of Democracy 21--who claimed any involvement in the drafting of the bill, and even he was unable to accurately answer questions about its effect. Of the eight amendments adopted by the Committee, four--including the 87-page substitute to the 84-page introduced bill--were to correct drafting errors apparently unnoticed in the three months from the Citizens United decision to the bill's introduction.

Among the errors implicitly acknowledged by the sponsors were a reversal of the Federal Election Commission's painstakingly crafted rule to allow free political speech on the Internet, a ban on PACs connected to companies employing over 5 million Americans and generating 6% of GDP, and a requirement that CEOs file a certification under penalty of perjury with the FEC before making any ``contribution, donation, [or] expenditure." Because the word ``donation" is not defined either in the Federal Election Campaign Act or the bill, that certification requirement apparently would have included charitable or civic donations as well as donations for state or local political activity where they are legal under state law.

Fortunately the majority accepted amendments from Representative McCarthy to correct some of these obvious errors. But the question remains what other consequences--intended or otherwise--have not yet been identified to be corrected. That question is particularly relevant because the substitute amendment was not provided to us until 22 hours before the beginning of the markup, hardly leaving time for a thorough review of its implications.

THE RUSH TO TAKE EFFECT

The bill becomes effective 30 days after its enactment, whether or not the Federal Election Commission has promulgated regulations. It is, of course, not possible either practically or consistent with the Administrative Procedure Act for regulations to be issued that quickly. This demonstrates a specific intent by the sponsors not only to rush the bill into effect to influence the outcome of the 2010 election, but to ignore the constitutional ramifications of imposing vague and complex restriction on political speech without any administrative clarification or instruction.

For example, Section 102 of the bill defines as a foreign national any corporation in which another foreign national ``directly or indirectly owns 20 percent or more of the voting shares." The phrase ``directly or indirectly" is not defined, leaving it to those who wish to express views on issues and candidates to determine whether it means corporations must look through institutional owners such as mutual funds and trusts to determine whether their ultimate owners are foreign nationals with ``indirect" interests. This analysis of multiple levels of ownership would be highly burdensome or even impossible, and the mere possibility that it is required likely would be enough to prevent speech. That, of course, appears to be precisely the sponsors' intent.

Even aside from institutional owners, companies would have to determine whether 20% or more of their shares are owned by foreign nationals as defined in the legislation. For a publicly-traded company this task would not only be difficult and expensive, but subject to constant change. The lack of any regulations or explanation on how to comply will mean the most likely outcome is, again, a decision not to speak for fear of violating a vague law. What chief executive will sign a certification under penalty of perjury when his counsel cannot advise what standard the certification will be judged against?

This problem extends beyond corporations trying to identify the nationality of their shareholders. The bill also defines as foreign nationals any corporation whose board of directors has a majority of foreign nationals. Many political committees of candidates and parties are incorporated entities. Under the standard set out in this bill, the chief executive of those committees will have to sign a certification under penalty of perjury that they do not have a majority of foreign nationals serving on the board of directors. To do this prudently, incorporated entities such as the Democratic National Committee and the Democratic Congressional Campaign Committee will have to ask each of their directors to verify their nationality--at least in the absence of a clarifying regulation from the FEC.

Sections 103 and 104 of the bill re-write rules governing coordinated activity--rules the FEC has been struggling to write consistent with the statute and the Constitution since BCRA passed in 2002. Again, the bill creates ambiguous standards for candidates and party committees and leaves no opportunity for clarification from the FEC.

There will be no opportunity for the FEC to issue regulations explaining the bill's wide-ranging and complex new disclosure requirements, nor to create forms that filers can use to comply with them. There will be no opportunity for the FEC to explain when the new advertising disclaimers are an unreasonable burden--leaving the speakers to guess and risk sanctions if they are wrong.

There is, of course, only one reason to rush this bill through the House and Senate and then rush it into effect--to alter the outcome of the 2010 election. The sponsors have been clear that is what they intend.[57]

Representative Harper offered an amendment to make the bill effective on January 1, 2011. This would give the FEC time to issue regulations and the courts time for at least an initial review of the bill's constitutionality in a preliminary injunction proceeding. It would also prevent the bill from being a tool to affect the outcome of the 2010 election. The majority rejected this amendment on a party-line vote.

If the intent to change election outcomes were not clear enough already, Section 401 makes it even clearer. Here the bill writes rules for judicial review that are different from both the Federal Election Campaign Act and the Bipartisan Campaign Reform Act, both of which are amended in this bill.

The result is not only the longest possible process for judicial review, but the possibility of lengthy collateral litigation to decide which of the three processes should apply.

So, in addition to the bill being rushed into effect, the opportunity for a court to review its compliance with the Constitution is delayed. This represents the maximum possible effort to leave unconstitutional provisions in effect as long as possible.

Because the judicial review provision is in the jurisdiction of another committee, we were not able to seek to amend it. Had we had the opportunity, we would have done so.

THE RUSH TO BAN SPEECH DIRECTLY

The sponsors of this bill like to describe it in gauzy, general terms as being about ``disclosure," and even went so far as to bestow that misleading label on it. However, the title of Section 101 begins ``Prohibiting independent expenditures and electioneering communications" and the title of Section 102 begins ``Application of the ban on contributions and expenditures." The bill explicitly and forthrightly bans certain entities from political speech, and it does so in a way that clearly is designed for partisan bias.

In its first substantive section, the bill bans independent expenditures and electioneering communications (which we will call ``political spending" or ``political expenditures") by companies holding a government contract worth $50,000 or more (an amount revised to $7,000,000 in the Committee markup). The bill claims in its findings that this will prevent government officials from influencing the contracting process based on political spending, and will prevent contractors from feeling pressure to make political expenditures.

What the bill ignores is that those arguments apply with equal or even greater force to unions representing government employees. Those unions negotiate directly with the government on the terms and conditions of employment, and their own revenues depend on having government employees pay them for this service. As such, union representatives have exactly the same incentives to influence contract decisions by government officials and exactly the same risks of being subjected to pressure to make political expenditures.

Despite this symmetry of potential for corruption or its appearance, the bill singles out corporate government contractors and ignores unions. Preventing quid pro quo corruption is the only remaining governmental interest sufficient to justify limitations on political speech. By ignoring this interest with respect to some speakers (unions) while emphasizing it with respect to others (business corporations), the majority undermines the constitutional basis of Congress' authority to act.

Representative Lungren offered an amendment to provide that the prohibition on political spending by government contractors would also apply to unions representing government employees.

The amendment was rejected on a party-line vote. Representative Lungren offered another amendment to provide that labor unions representing employees of government contractors would be covered by the ban in the same way as the contractors themselves. That amendment also was rejected on a party-line vote.

Other recipients of government funds are subject to the same possibility of corruption as contractors. This concern is shown by the bill's ban on political spending by TARP recipients, and applies with equal force to recipients of government grants. Grantees may also make political expenditures to influence the grant-award process or feel pressured to make expenditures in return for receiving grants.

Recognizing this, Representative Harper offered an amendment to prohibit organizational recipients of federal funds (such as ACORN) from making political expenditures. The amendment was rejected. The second substantive section of the bill bans political spending by an expanded range of foreign nationals. Proponents of the bill use the example of foreign sovereign wealth funds to justify expanding the existing limits on foreign activity in American elections. Recognizing this concern, Representative Lungren offered an amendment to replace the bill's language on foreign nationals with a simpler, more enforceable two-part section. The first part would codify the existing FEC regulation prohibiting foreign nationals making decision on spending to influence American elections. The second would ban political spending by entities majority-owned by a foreign government or political party. The amendment was rejected.

Because the description of sovereign wealth funds in the amendment was questioned, he then proposed adopting the first part of the amendment, codifying the current FEC regulatory prohibition. That amendment was rejected on a party-line vote.

While the bill prohibits political spending by corporations based on the nationality of their owners or directors, it includes no similar provisions to ensure that the massive political spending by labor unions is untainted by foreign influence. To correct this disparity, Representative Lungren proposed an amendment to require that union chief executives make a certification similar to that required of corporate chief executives attesting that no dues in the union treasury funding the political spending were received from foreign nationals. This amendment was rejected on a party-line vote.

The majority opposed the amendment based on the burden it would impose on unions to verify the citizenship status of the members whose funds would be used for political expenditures--yet the majority refused to recognize the burden on corporations of verifying the citizenship status of shareholders to determine whether the foreign nationals exceed the bill's 20% threshold.

Because of the potential for conflicts when government officials and funds are used to collect money to be used for political spending, Representative McCarthy offered an amendment stating that funds obtained by a union through a government-administered payroll deduction program may not be used for political expenditures.[58] The majority rejected this amendment on a party-line vote.

The Committee's consideration of the bill showed a clear pattern. The underlying language bans speech by a specific class of organizations, corporations. When we sought to at least make the bans even-handed by applying them to unions, the majority rejected the efforts again and again. The majority's refusal to make the bill apply evenly to all speakers sets it on a collision course with the clear holding of the Supreme Court just four months ago: ``We find no basis for the proposition that, in the context of political speech, the Government may impose restrictions on certain disfavored speakers."[59]

THE RUSH TO BAN SPEECH INDIRECTLY

The bill's sponsors appear to believe that by making disclosure its most prominent--and even eponymous--purpose they can perform an act of legerdemain and convince people that its purpose really is disclosure. No one should be fooled.

Under current law, most organizations that engage in the political process already are subject to extensive reporting and disclosure requirements. Political committees--including candidate committees, party committees, PACs, and others--must report regularly to the FEC on their receipt and disbursement of funds. They must itemize contributions from donors giving more than $200 per year. In most cases they must file electronically, and as the election becomes closer their reports become more frequent. Groups organized under section

527 of the IRS code, if they are not already covered in the category above, must file as though they were political committees.

In addition to these entities that must report all of their activity regularly to the FEC, anyone making an expenditure for an independent expenditure (over $250) or an electioneering communication (over $10,000) must report that expenditure to the FEC. In sum, there is no shortage of reporting and disclosure required under current law.

With political committees and 527s covered by existing law and 501(c)(3) charitable organizations banned from political activity, the remaining targets of this bill's disclosure requirements are 501(c)(4) social welfare organizations and 501(c)(6) trade associations. While these organizations are permitted to make political expenditures under the tax code and retain their tax-exempt status, such expenditures may not be their primary activity. As such, 501(c) organizations by definition are engaged in extensive non-political activities that form their primary activity and establish their identity (shown, for example, by the clearly identified interests of 501(c)(4) organizations such as the Sierra Club and the National Rifle Association). The sponsors have not explained why this identity is not enough information for voters, and must be supplemented by delving into the organizations' sources of funds--especially when donations identified for use in political spending already must be disclosed.

This very effort to force disclosure of sources of funds raises serious constitutional concerns. The Supreme Court found in NAACP v. Alabama that the government could not compel these organizations to reveal their donors publicly; the only exception to this rule has been where the donation is given specifically for use in a political expenditure. The bill turns this presumption on its head--the new rule is that donations above a certain amount must be disclosed unless they are specifically excluded from use for political expenditures.

In an effort to avoid this constitutional limitation, the bill's authors create a new category or political entity with reporting obligations: the ``Campaign Related Activity Account'' (``CRAA''). Depending on a convoluted set of circumstances, the threshold above which disclosure is required may be $6,000 or $10,000 if an organization established a CRAA and $600 or $1,000 if it does not. In an effort to partially mitigate the new compliance burden of this system and slightly reduce the legal thicket one must navigate to comply with the campaign finance law, Representative McCarthy offered an amendment to set the disclosure threshold for organizations with a CRAA at the same level as the current threshold for itemized disclosure by political committees. This amendment was rejected on a party-line vote. The most likely effect of this bill's disclosure regime is not to provide the public with useful information, but to impose still-higher compliance costs and deter political speech. Indeed, from the statements of the sponsors it appears that is precisely the intent. We commend attention to the detailed critique of this regime in the letter from eight former FEC commissioners that is part of the markup record. We also condemn the use of a salutary goal--disclosure of money spent to influence politics--to conceal an effort that is actually designed to stifle political speech for partisan gain.

The bill includes another attempt to stifle speech that masquerades as adding information for the public. The new ``stand by your ad'' requirement for organizations making political expenditures gives every appearance of being designed to restrict speech. The rule is modeled on one in BCRA for candidates. In a 2007 article, Bob Bauer (then a campaign finance lawyer for Democrats including candidate Barack Obama, now the White House Counsel) said of the BCRA rule, ``this requirement makes sense only if its true use is clearly identified: to regulate the content of ads."[60] Bauer argues that the disclosure provides no benefit to the audience, which assumes the ad is approved by the candidate who paid for it.

Likewise, existing law will require the sponsors subject to this bill's ``stand by your ad" rule to disclose that they paid for the ad, so there is no added disclosure benefit to the viewer.

On the other hand, the disclosures required in this bill are exceptionally onerous. The head of an organization paying for an ad must identify himself or herself by name and title and state the name of the organization twice. If there is a ``significant funder" that person must also identify himself or herself by name and title and state the name of their organization three times. The result can be--in addition to the currently required disclosure of who paid for the ad--two names, two titles, and no fewer than five recitations of organizational names. One could reasonably expect this to consume more than half of a 30-second ad, and our experiments show that indeed it does.

In the substitute amendment offered by the majority there is a feeble attempt to mitigate this burden on speech by calling on the FEC to promulgate regulations to determine when the disclaimer constitutes a hardship by consuming a disproportionate amount of the ad's content. This is another example of the bill's politically-motivated sleight-of-hand--the disclaimer rule becomes effective 30 days after enactment, but this hardships exemption is not effective until the FEC issues regulations. Thus the exemption is likely to be nonexistent during the 2010 elections.

In his testimony before this Committee, former United States Solicitor General Theodore B. Olson said, ``When we are going to restrict the ability of individuals in this country to speak and make it a crime if they get it wrong, we have a very solemn obligation to make it very, very clear." This statement emphasizes the critical importance of campaign finance laws that are clear and easily understood--a standard this bill badly fails to meet. The Supreme Court has said ``political speech . . . is central to the meaning and purpose of the First Amendment."[61] When legislating in the area, Congress must not be so vague or impose rules so burdensome that it infringes this core constitutional right.

The Rush to Complicate Speech

At the Committee's February 3 hearing on Citizens United decision, members from both parties supported the idea of increasing or eliminating the limit on political party spending done in coordination with candidates. The members noted that the funds spent would still be ``hard money" subject to the source and amount limitations in the Federal Election Campaign Act and that lifting the limit would give candidates a ready and non-corrupting source of support if they were targeted by an attack. Making this change is a simple revision to the statute. The bill's authors turned it into eight pages of text redefining terms and creating new rules and exceptions and doing, frankly, we know not what else.

In the first hearing on this bill on May 6, Representative Lungren asked a witness who had stated he was involved in drafting the bill whether the new definition of ``coordinated communication" meant that a candidate could be liable for accepting an excessive contribution based on activity the candidate knew nothing about, if someone republished the candidate's campaign material without the candidate's knowledge. The witness hemmed, hawed, and ultimately insisted the language in the bill is the same as that in existing law.

It is true that words appear in existing law, but they appear in a section that states republication of campaign material is an expenditure. This is significantly different from stating that it is--alone, with nothing else--a coordinated communication and therefore a contribution. In the face of this testimony, we can only conclude that even the bill's authors do not understand it.

Representative Lungren offered an amendment to do exactly and only what the members from both parties discussed at the February 3 hearing--remove the limit on expenditures made by a party in coordination with a candidate. The amendment was rejected.

CONCLUSION

This bill is both a smokescreen to adopt still more restrictions on political speech in the name of ``reform'' and an attempt to use Citizens United as a smokescreen to stifle criticism of Democrats in order to help their candidates retain office in the 2010 election.

More than half of the majority's witnesses at hearings on this bill said the real solution is not disclosure but taxpayer financing of congressional campaigns. At the markup of the bill Representative Capuano proposed an amendment to do just that, based on a bill whose cost is estimated at nearly $1 billion annually to fund campaigns for Congress.

The bill itself shows a consistent pattern of restricting corporate speech and allowing unions to proceed unhindered. For instance, the $600 disclosure threshold in the bill appears to be just above the annual dues of most union members--meaning unions will have no additional disclosure obligations. That is in addition to being exempt outright from the bill's bans on political spending. The bill's sponsors said repeatedly that they intend the bill to affect the 2010 elections and they intend it to limit political speech.

Perhaps the Chicago Tribune summarized H.R. 5175 best:

``Though DISCLOSE has some tolerable provisions, it is on the whole a vast and unconstitutional infringement on a key American freedom.'' This is a deeply flawed bill. It deserves vigorous and forthright opposition and prompt defeat.

Daniel E. Lungren.
Kevin McCarthy.
Gregg Harper.

End Notes

[1] Coates, John, ``Statement before the U.S. House of Representatives' Committee on House Administration,'' May 11, 2010.

[2] Kenneth P. Doyle, Outside Groups' Spending Crosses Line Into `Express Advocacy' Ads in House Race, BNA Money and Politics Report, May 14, 2010; see also ``Testimony of the Brennan Center at NYU School of Law before the Committee on House Administration, U.S. House of Representatives'' May 11, 2010, available at http://www.brennancenter.org/page/-/Democracy/CFR/BCtestimonyDISCLOSEact.pdf?nocdn=1.

[3] Wertheimer, Fred, ``Pro & Con: Is the Supreme Court's Ruling on Campaigns bad for Democracy?'', Atlanta Journal-Constitution: January 27, 2010.

[4] Joseph Weber, ``Candidates cut back bucks for Hill seats,'' Washington Times: May 18, 2010.

[5] ``U.S. Election Will Cost $5.3 Billion, Center for Responsive Politics Predicts," Center for Responsive Politics: October 22, 2008.

[6] Voters believe it is important to know the identity of sponsors of ads in making decisions. See McConnell v. FEC, 251 F. Supp. 176, 231 (D.D.C. 2003) (quoting David B. Magleby, Report Concerning Interest Group Electioneering Advocacy and Party Soft Money Activity) (``Voters, when asked, have consistently indicated that they would like to know who it is that is conducting electioneering. In 2000 voters in Montana faced a competitive U.S. Senate and a competitive U.S. House race. A late October Montana State University-Billings Poll found that, 78 percent of the survey respondents reported that it was ``very" or ``somewhat important" for them to know who ``pays for or sponsors a political ad." Our focus group participants in 2000 had very similar views on the question of the importance of their knowing who is paying for or sponsoring an ad. More than four-fifths (81%) said it was very or somewhat important to know the identity of the sponsor. In the national Knowledge Networks Survey in 2000, 78 percent said the same thing.").

[7] For example, the Committee is aware that in the 2006 California state controller's race, Intuit, a software corporation that distributes the ``Turbo Tax" software program, funneled $1 million through a group called the Alliance for California Tomorrow, which made independent expenditures in support of a state controller who opposed the creation of a free-on-line tax preparation program for California residents. In Florida's 2006 gubernatorial primary, the U.S. Sugar Corporation funneled approximately $1 million in independent expenditures through deceptively-named fronts--``Florida's Working Families" and ``The Coalition for Justice and Equality. In a 2007 Colorado ballot measure election, a group called ``Littleton Neighbors Voting No" spent $170,000 to defeat a zoning restriction that would have prevented a new Walmart. When the disclosure reports for these groups were filed, it was revealed that ``Littleton Neighbors" was exclusively funded by Walmart. See Testimony of the Brennan Center for Justice at NYU School of Law before the House Committee on Administration, May 11, 2010; Dennis J. Ventry Jr., Intuit Uses Clout to Stymie State Innovation, Sacramento Bee, Oct. 6, 2009 (also see Campaign Finance Reports for Intuit and Alliance for California Tomorrow, available at http://cal- access.ss.ca.gov/default.aspx). Several other examples of ``veiled" corporate and union spending are provided in Elizabeth Garrett & Daniel A. Smith, Veiled Political Actors and Campaign Disclosure Laws in Direct Democracy, 4 Election L.J. 295 (2005).

[8] Holman, Craig, ``Statement before the U.S. House of Representatives' Committee on House Administration," May 6, 2010 (explaining that most corporations are likely to funnel their political expenditures through intermediaries, namely, 501(c) nonprofit groups and section 527s with the same electoral agenda.)

[9] See Elizabeth Garrett & Daniel A. Smith, Veiled Political Actors and Campaign Disclosure Laws in Direct Democracy, 4 Election L.J. 295, 305 (2005). Anonymous spenders can also avoid reputational harm from taking political positions that some voters (or, in the case of certain corporations, customers and shareholders) may not like. See id.

[10] See generally 251 F. Supp. 2d 176, 227-33, 438-537 (D.D.C. 2003) (findings of fact in court's per curiam opinion and findings of fact by Judge Kollar-Kotelly); see also id. at 231(D.D.C. 2003) (quoting David B. Magleby, Report Concerning Interest Group Electioneering Advocacy and Party Soft Money Activity) (``[t]he current system places an unreasonable burden on voters to ascertain who is attempting to persuade them in an election. Our focus groups and survey data from 2000 show that to voters, party and interest group electioneering advertisements are indistinguishable from candidate advertisements. . . . Even the candidates and their campaign managers are unable to ascertain who some of the groups running ads were. . . . And in the CSED national survey, I found that respondents were often confused as to whether party ads were paid for by candidates or parties.").

[11] See id. at 542-43.

[12] Id.; see also id. at 545 (``It is clear that The Coalition's issue advocacy campaign was designed to influence the 1996 general election and was accomplished through candidate-centered issue advocacy so as to avoid FECA's source and disclosure limitations.") (opinion of Kollar-Kotelly, J.).

[13] Id. at 545.

[14] Id.; see also id. at 546 (citing evidence from the record that CBM described itself as ``a grassroots organization representing the interests of patients, seniors, disabled Americans, small businesses, pharmaceutical research companies and many others concerned with Medicare reform.")

[15] Id. at 201.

[16] Id.

[17] Annenberg Public Policy Center, Issue Advertising in the 1999-2000 Election Cycle at 2.

[18] Id. at 1.

[19] See 251 F. Supp.2d at 229.

[20] Id. at 229-230 (quoting Declaration of Terry S. Beckett).

[21] Gilbert, Lisa ``Statement before the U.S. House of Representatives' Committee on House Administration," May 6, 2010.

[22] Holman, Craig, ``Statement before the U.S. House of Representatives' Committee on House Administration," May 6, 2010 ( urging that the ``enhancement of transparency alone makes this measure a valuable response to the Citizens United decision that Congress should approve without delay.")

[23] Coates, John, ``Statement before the U.S. House of Representatives' Committee on House Administration," May 11, 2010 (explaining that ``Investors will be able to learn the level of new political activity permitted by Citizens United in the companies in which they invest. They can look for patterns consistent with managerial pursuit of private interests. If patterns are found, they can engage in self-help, by selling their shares, by suing managers for `waste' of corporate assets or by proposing bylaw amendments to directly control political activity, or if managers act particularly egregiously, to pressure boards to discipline managers."

[24] See Elizabeth Garrett & Daniel A. Smith, Veiled Political Actors and Campaign Disclosure Laws in Direct Democracy, 4 Election L.J. 295, 327 (2005).

[25] A 2008 survey of corporate directors found that 88% agreed with the proposition that corporations should be required to publicly disclose all corporate funds used for political purposes, and a majority of directors (57%) likewise disagreed with the proposition that additional reporting requirements and transparency in corporate political spending would be too burdensome and costly. Mason-Dixon Polling and Research, 2008 Nationwide Survey of Members of Corporate Boards of Directors.

[26] See, e.g., Norman J. Ornstein and Thomas E. Mann, eds. The Permanent Campaign and its Future. Washington, D.C.: American Enterprise Institute Press, 2000, at vii (``Candidates for the presidency and Congress are now in a perpetual campaign mode. . . . The line between campaigning and governing has all but disappeared, with campaigning increasingly dominant."). See also ``In Campaign 2008, Candidates Starting Earlier, Spending More," Washington Post, Feb. 7, 2007.

[27] Simon, Donald, ``Statement before the U.S. House of Representatives' Committee on House Administration," May 6, 2010.

[28] Potter, Trevor, ``Statement before the U.S. House of Representatives' Committee on House Administration," May 11, 2010 (urging Congress to require complete disclosure in time for the 2010 elections).

[29] Citizens United v. FEC, 558 U.S._, 55 (2010).

[30] See, e.g., Elizabeth Garrett & Daniel A. Smith, Veiled Political Actors and Campaign Disclosure Laws in Direct Democracy (2005); Noel M. Murray, et al., Public Policy Relating to Consumer Comprehension of Television Commercials: A Review and Some Empirical Results (1993).

[31] Citizens United, at 55.

[32] Id. at 51

[33] Id. at 53.

[34] 2 U.S.C. Sec. 441c.

[35] 11 C.F.R. Sec. 115.2(a).

[36] The Federalist NO. 3 (John Jay) (``At present I mean only to consider it as it respects security for the preservation of peace and tranquility, as well as against dangers from foreign arms and influence, as from dangers of the like kind arising from domestic causes. . . . Let us therefore proceed to examine whether the people are not right in their opinion that a cordial Union, under an efficient national government, affords them the best security that can be devised against hostilities from abroad.").

[37] Foreign Agents Registration Act Amendments of 1966, Pub. L. No. 89-486, 80 Stat. 244; S. Rep. No. 89-143 (1965).

[38] S. Rep. No. 105-167 (1998).

[39] See, e.g., U.S. v. Kanchanalak, 192 F.3d 1037 (D.C. Cir. 1999) (defendants disguised illegal contributions from foreign nationals).

[40] 2 U.S.C. Sec. 441e.

[41] Citizens United, 130 S. Ct. at 911.

[42] Lynch, Elizabeth, ``Statement before the U.S. House of Representatives' Committee on House Administration," May 11, 2010 (noting that for foreign corporations doing business in the United States, it is common to establish a U.S. subsidiary corporation.

[43] Holman, Craig, ``Statement before the U.S. House of Representatives' Committee on House Administration," May 6, 2010.

[44] See ``SOI Tax Stats--Foreign-Controlled Domestic Corporations," found at http://www.irs.gov/ taxstats/bustaxstats/ article/0,,id=96311,00.html.

[45] ``Foreign Ownership of U.S. Companies Jumps," Reuters, Aug. 27, 2008.

[46] See Jeff May, InBev completes purchase of Anheuser-Busch, New Jersey Business News, November 18, 2008, available at http://www.nj.com/business/index.ssf/2008/11/inbev_completes_purchase_of_an.html; 7-Eleven Profile, available at http://www.7- eleven.com/NewsRoom/Background Information/7Eleven Profile/tabid/164/Default.aspx; http://www.benjerry.com/company/sear/2008/sear08_4.0.cfm; http://www.hoovers.com/company/T-Mobile_Usa_Inc/hskkri_1.html.

[47] Lynch, Elizabeth, ``Statement before the U.S. House of Representatives' Committee on House Administration," May 11, 2010.

[48] Coates, John, ``Statement before the U.S. House of Representatives' Committee on House Administration," May 11, 2010; Lynch, Elizabeth, ``Statement before the U.S. House of Representatives' Committee on House Administration," May 11, 2010.

[49] See http://www.opensecrets.org/pacs/foreign.php. See also Stephanie Kirchgaessner, BAE Among Top Foreign Donors to U.S. Political Candidates, Financial Times, August 22, 2006 (``BAE, the British defence group, has emerged as one of the most powerful corporate contributors to candidates in the current U.S. election cycle, ranking number 18 in a list of the biggest corporate donors."); U.S. Elections Got More Foreign Cash--PAC's of Overseas Companies Gave $2.3 Million in 1986 Congress Campaigns, N.Y. Times, A27 (May 24, 1987); Tom Hamburger & Greg Gordon, U.S. Foreign Policy is Target of a World of Political Donors: Millions Linked to Other Countries, Minneapolis-St. Paul Star-Trib., Mar. 16, 1997, at 21A.

[50] T he Department of Justice posts FARA records at http://www.justice.gov/criminal/fara/links/quick-search.html.

[51] Dan Eggen, BP is getting more political, and that may help weather oil-spill storm, Wash. Post, May 6, 2010, at A17; John M. Biers, Activists Say BP Breaking Promise On Campaign Donations, Dow Jones Energy Service, Nov. 7, 2006, available at http://www.politicalaccountability.net/index.php?ht=display/ Article Details/ i/1209/pid/188. For state expenditure data, see http://www.followthemoney.org.

[52] ``Foreign Ownership of U.S. Companies Jumps," Reuters, Aug. 27, 2008.

[53] As has been recognized in state corporations law, individuals who hold 20% or more of the voting shares of a company frequently exercise de facto control of the company. See 8 Del. C. Sec. 203(c)(4). Even in circumstances where such individuals do not exercise de facto control, they possess significant and perceptible influence over the company's decisions.

[54] Coates, John, ``Statement before the U.S. House of Representatives' Committee on House Administration," May 11, 2010.

[55] Simon, Donald, ``Statement before the U.S. House of Representatives' Committee on House Administration," May 6, 2010 (testifying that ``The Court in Citizens United was clear that it believed the key hedge against quid pro quo corruption resulting from campaign-related corporate spending is the requirement that such spending be independent of, i.e., not coordinated with, the candidate who is benefitted."

[56] Simon, Donald, ``Statement before the U.S. House of Representatives' Committee on House Administration," May 6, 2010.

[57] See, e.g., ``New Rules Proposed on Campaign Donors," The Wall Street Journal, Feb. 12, 2010 (``[Sen. Schumer] said he hoped the proposed legislation would discourage companies and unions from spending freely on political advertisements. The disclosure requirements `will make them think twice,' before attempting to influence election outcomes, he said, adding, `The deterrent effect should not be underestimated.'") and ``Castle, Jones Back Van Hollen Bill," Politico, April 28, 2010 (``Van Hollen has said he's hopeful the bill could be implemented in time to affect newly legal ad spending in 2010 congressional races.").

[58] The United States Court of Appeals upheld a similar provision against a federal constitutional challenge in Toledo Area AFL-CIO Council v. Pizza, 154 F.3d 307 (6th Cir., 1998).

[59] Citizens United v. Federal Election Comm'n, 558 U.S._, No. 08-205, slip op. at 25 (Jan. 21, 2010).

[60] ``Disclosure in an Expanded Regulatory System," 6 Election Law Journal 38, 45-46 (2007).

[61] Citizens United v. Federal Election Comm'n, 558 U.S.__, No. 08-205, slip op. at 12 (Jan. 21, 2010).

INDEX

A

B

C

Q

R

S

T

U

V

W